Stonehenge

and

Druidism

by

E. RAYMOND CAPT M.A., A.I.A., F.S.A. Scot.

Archaeological Institute of America

COVER DESIGN AND ORIGINAL ILLUSTRATIONS BY J.A. DRYBURGH

PUBLISHED BY

HOFFMAN PRINTING CO.
P.O. Box 1529
Muskogee, Oklahoma 74402
(918) 682-8341
www.artisanpublishers.com

ISBN 0-934666-04-0
Library of Congress catalog card number: 79-54773

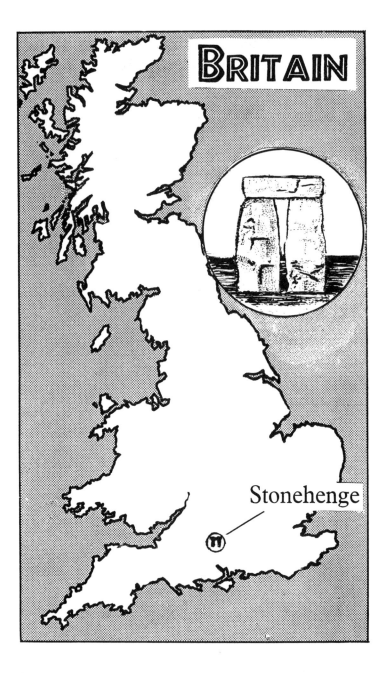

BRITAIN

Stonehenge

PREFACE

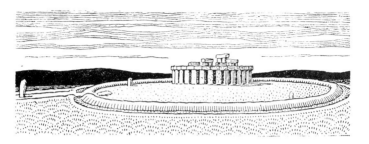

Stonehenge — standing in lonely majesty on England's great Salisbury Plain — is wreathed in mystery. From the earliest times, it has aroused the awe and curiosity of its visitors. What was its purpose? Who were the master builders? When was it built?

Although not counted as one of the seven wonders of the ancient world, Stonehenge is one of the most unique wonders of the world. A monument so old that its true history was probably forgotten by classic times. Greek and Roman writers hardly mentioned it.

There have been many folk legends and stories attached to that "Gigantic Pile" as it was called by ancient writers. In more modern times most scholars agree it served as some kind of ceremonial building or religious structure for ancient peoples. It is, however, only within the last century, that archaeological excavations and astronomical computations have yielded reliable information about its origin, history and purpose.

From pottery shards, ancient burials and the silent stones themselves, have come the amazing saga of a race of colonizers who created a unique civilization, in Britain, over 2000 years before the birth of Christ.

Stonehenge stands today, one signpost left along the way that identifies the Building Race. It bears witness to the vigour and vitality of a national religion, already passed from the primitive into the metaphysical stage, which embodied abstract ideas, astronomical observations and a high and pure code of ethics.

3

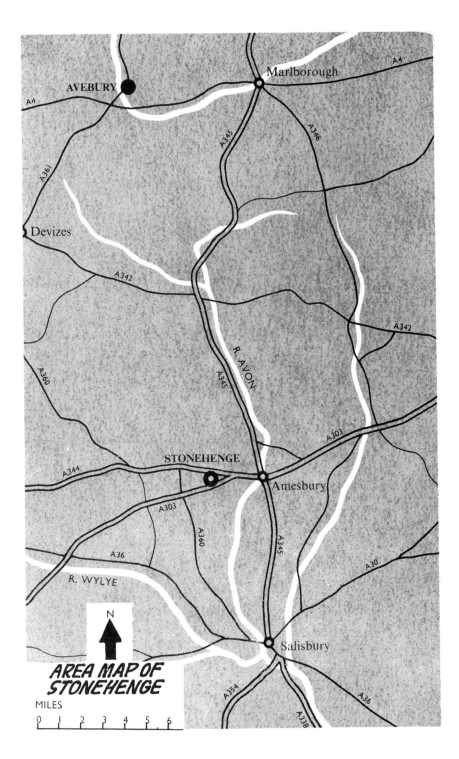

AVEBURY

Marlborough

A4

A4

A345

A346

A361

Devizes

A342

A342

A360

R. AVON

A345

A303

STONEHENGE

A344

Amesbury

A303

A360

A345

A303

A36

A30

R. WYLYE

N

AREA MAP OF
STONEHENGE

MILES

0 1 2 3 4 5 6

Salisbury

A354

A36

A338

LEGENDARY RECORD

Known in ancient times as the place of the "hanging stones," Stonehenge has defied, alike, the winds and rains of 4000 years and the probing questions of historian and archaeologist. The origin of Stonehenge, being lost in the mists of time, resulted in the necessity of creating a biography. So – man invented some fanciful legends.

The identity of the first such biographer is not known, but by the twelfth century A.D. Stonehenge was well wrapped in speculation and legend. An early story relates how Merlin the Wizard aided in the building of Stonehenge which was built to commemorate the massacre of several hundred British princes.

By the end of the 17th century, the building of Stonehenge had been attributed, in turn, to the Greeks, Romans, Danes and Phoenicians. In the mid-1800s an article appeared, titled, "An Unprejudicial, Authentic and Interesting Account which that Stupendous and Beautiful Edifice Stonehenge, in Wiltshire, is Found to Give of Itself." The writer, named Henry Browne of Amesbury, reached the conclusion that the Stonehenge stones had been erected during the days of Adam and knocked down by the Flood. He offered, as clinching proof of his hypothesis, the fact that most of the Stonehenge dilapidation is now on the southwest side: "...the waters of the Deluge advanced against Stonehenge...from...the southwest."

In 1883, one W. S. Blacket theorized that the creators of the mysterious structure were not from any known land, but were the mythical people of the Lost Continent, Atlantis via the New World: "The Apalacian Indians with their priests and medicine men, must have been the builders of Stonehenge..."

DRAWING OF STONEHENGE

A year after Blacket had introduced Atlantis, the last of the fanciful nineteenth century speculations was advanced by another writer, named T. A. Wise. He suggested Stonehenge was one of the "high places of the Druids," until it fell into the hands of Buddhist Missionaries.

In 1889 Professor A.T. Evans wrote (Archaeological Review) that Stonehenge was an advanced representation of sepulchral architecture, "where the cult or worship of departed ancestors may have become associated with the worship of the Celtic Zeus; the form under which the divinity was worshipped would have been that of his sacred oak."

The most popular theory, still believed by many, is that Stonehenge was built by Druidic Priests of the pagan Celts who invaded Britain before the birth of Christ. Although the Druids were not the actual builders, they were seemingly familiar with its purpose and used Stonehenge as an open air sanctuary.

Stonehenge remained a mystery until early in the present century. Then it was realized; only a more objective archaeological investigation of the site might solve this ancient British riddle. And early in the present century such investigation began. Today, much of the mystery of Stonehenge has been cleared away.

OLD ENGRAVING OF STONEHENGE

PHYSICAL APPEARANCE

Stonehenge is a circle of monoliths, on the Salisbury Plain, about 60 miles southwest of London and about 8 miles north of Salisbury. It stands on an almost level area of a slight eminence of the treeless chalk downs. To the west, the ground rises slightly; in all other directions it falls, though gently. The steepest slope is on the east, where it descends to the floor of a dry valley.

The first glimpse is often keenly disappointing, for the stones, immense as they are, seem entirely dwarfed by the vast background of rolling Wiltshire Downs. It is not until one approaches more closely, and views the stones, silhouetted against the sky, that the true size of the monument becomes apparent.

The variety of texture and color of the stones themselves, that changes with shifting light and shade, adds to the magnificence and picturesque effect. From a distance, they have a silvery-grey color in sunlight, which lightens to an almost metallic bluish-white against a background of storm clouds. When the ground is covered by snow in midwinter, with a dull leaden sky threatening further falls, they seem nearly black; and at sunset in midsummer their surfaces glow, as if from within, with a soft warm pinkish-orange light.

Upon closer examination, each stone takes on its own individual pattern of color and texture. The shades of color range from off-white through soft buff or pink, to a dull mat-grey. Here and there, patches of fluffy grey-green lichen, accented by vivid spots of scaly yellow, add highlights to this masterpiece in stone.

On many of the surfaces, the stones are streaked and lined by close-set vertical cracks and fissures, like the grain of some vast stump of a petrified tree. Eroded hollows and overhangs create a timeless permanence that sets Stonehenge apart from all other early prehistoric monuments.

Although nearly obliterated by the scouring forces of wind and rain, the signs of man's handiwork are everywhere apparent: the squared and tapered forms of the stones: the severely functional shapes of the mortice and tenon joints on the uprights and lintels: and the delicate, rippled fluting of their tooled surfaces. This evidence of the hand of the mason allows us to confer upon Stonehenge the dignity of architecture, in contrast to many other early monuments whose stones were only chosen, but not shaped, by man.

The most prominent feature of Stonehenge is a 97 foot, 4 inch ring of 20 to 40 ton uprights and horizontal slabs (known as the Sarsen Circle) surrounding five huge trilithons archways, forming a horse-shoe. Inside the sarsen horseshoe are found blue colored stones that once formed another circle and horseshoe. In the center is yet another blue stone, now buried in the ground beneath the fallen stones of the great sarsen trilithon.

Today, the surfaces of the Sarsens bear undoubted signs of weather, but there is evidence that originally they were beautifully finished with rough tooling covering their surface. In the process of raising one of the Trilithon uprights a thin slab of that part of the stone, which had been buried in the foundation, became detached. The tooling upon this fragment was found to be perfect and as clean and sharp as when it left the hand of the craftsman, about four thousand years ago. Experiments to duplicate the workmanship found that quartzite pebbles, used as a tool, at once reproduced the character and surface of the fragment.

Just outside the Sarsen Circle occur two concentric rings of pits, known as the Y and Z holes. The Z holes range from 5 to 15 feet outside the Sarsen Circle and the Y holes are about 35 feet away. They are not arranged on true circles. Unfortunately, these holes are not marked on the ground today.

The outer boundary of Stonehenge is a low bank which lies about 100 feet outside the Sarsen Circle. Originally, it stood about 6 feet high and consisted of chalk rubble quarried from the ditch immediately outside it. Erosion, by weathering, has caused most of it to slip back into the ditch. A broad gap in the earthwork, on the northeast side, provided the entrance to the complex, although there are various smaller gaps, elsewhere; some made in modern times.

Just inside the bank there is a concentric ring of 56 pits, now filled in, known as the Aubrey Holes, named after their 17th century discoverer, John Aubrey. Two mounds straddle the Aubrey Holes circle. These are known as the North Barrow and the South Barrow.

From the entrance, an ancient roadway known as the Avenue, runs downhill, northeast, to the River Avon at West Amesbury, about two miles away. The Avenue is bound by a small bank and ditch, on either side. At the entrance of the earthwork is a large fallen stone, known as the "Slaughter Stone." It originally stood upright together with a similar stone, now missing to form a ceremonial doorway to the site.

Some 100 feet outside the entrance, and in the Avenue, was erected a third stone, now known as the "Heel Stone". A narrow ditch, filled with chalk, surrounds the Heel Stone. Nearby are four small holes and two larger holes; all are now filled in with chalk.

The Heel Stone is a large undressed stone, somewhat pointed at the top. Although probably erected in a straight-up position, it now leans inward toward the circle at an angle of about 30 degrees from the perpendicular. It is possibly the first stone erected at Stonehenge.

RECONSTRUCTION OF STONEHENGE

Just how the Heel Stone came by its name is not known for certain. It is supposed that the name was first used by John Aubrey, who described a certain stone as having a large depression shaped like a "Friar's heel." (Such an indentation is not found on the stone)

11

THE HEEL STONE

LOOKING NORTH

EARLY PEOPLE

For thousands of years, up to about 4000 B.C., the population of Britain consisted of scattered bands of roving hunters, living on wild game and wild plants. They apparently grew no crops, had no domesticated animals, and left behind them nothing but a few examples of their simple stone tools and flint weapons. These must be sought after with patient and expert care.

Many of the stone implements have been found in gravel terraces, particularly in the south of England, perhaps lost on ancient hunting expeditions, or hidden and forgotten among the riverside vegetation.

Lost or discarded tools and flint chippings have been found in some natural caves, where (it is assumed) those ancient hunters took shelter, in the winter months, when they could not follow the game herds. The flint implements were formed from flint nodules, trimmed to shape by removing small chips from the surface, or they were shaped from rough flakes struck from a nodule. All were multi-purpose tools for cutting and shaping wood, killing game, preparing skins, digging for vegetable foods and other functions.

Often searchers of Stone Age implements find the bones of elephants, hippopotami, mammoths, bears and other great beasts that lived in England during the alternating warm and arctic phases of the Ice Age.

FLINT DISCS OR SCRAPERS

FLINT CORES

FLINT HAND AXES

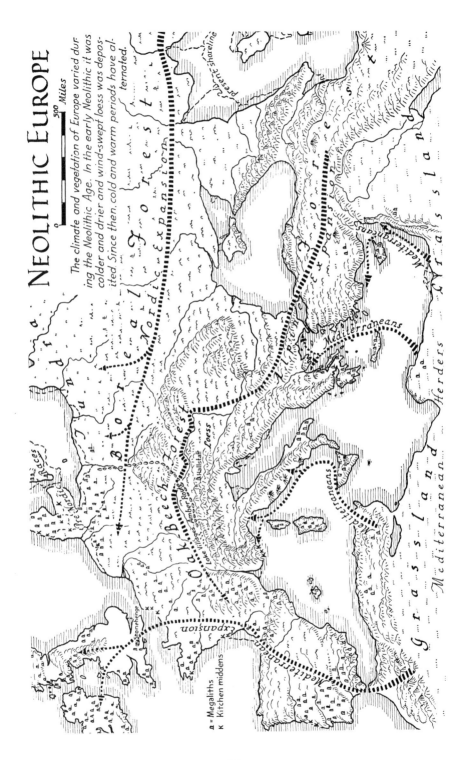

Neolithic Europe

0   500 Miles

The climate and vegetation of Europe varied during the Neolithic Age. In the early Neolithic it was colder and drier and wind-swept loess was deposited. Since then, cold and warm periods have alternated.

a = Megaliths
K Kitchen middens

Then, there came a time when a milder climate allowed first pine and then oak forests to spread across Europe. There the native peoples, still dependent on wild foods, often lived by the sea shore or river banks where they could supplement their diet with substantial amounts of fish and other sea life. Such a way of life could hardly produce lasting monuments. Only a few huts and marsh-side dwellings have been excavated. These are of a kind which can be excavated but not preserved.

Megalithic monuments began to appear in Spain and Western Europe around 3500 B.C. They were related to both religion and burials. In different forms, these megalithic graves and accompanying religions spread from the western Mediterranean, northwards, through France, Brittany and the British Isles, to northern Germany and Scandinavia. When they came to the north, the megalithic builders found already living there, people of an earlier Neolithic culture, known from their pottery as the "funnel-beaker" culture. These people buried their dead in small "cists" or boxes.

Although our knowledge of the early megalithic builders is still scanty, a study of the monuments they left and the objects found in them has allowed the archaeologists to identify the various periods by their distinguishing features. Each separate period had been assigned an identifying name. These megalithic builders brought with them the arts of growing grain and breeding cattle. In many countries, their arrival seems to have brought no corresponding change in tools and pottery, which continued to be made by methods previously in use. This would indicate that there had been no general change in the population and their intrusion was brought about without the use of force or invasion.

These first peaceful invasions were followed by others, bringing varying but related building techniques and culture. Assimilation of native pre-existent cultures and the passage of time brought about separate cultural development in the different countries.

The first of the megalithic builders to enter Britain crossed from France and the Low Countries to the south and southeast coasts and

15

the downs of Wessex. They brought with them domestic cattle, sheep and pigs and the seed grain of wheat and barley. Tending their cattle herds and cultivating a primitive form of wheat on scattered patches of ground, they led a simple and apparently peaceful existence. These earliest farming colonists are known as the "Windmill People" (Primary Neolithic). They built the "causewayed camps" (large hilltop enclosures) like Windmill Hill, the earthen long barrows and the Cursus monuments, like the one near Stonehenge.

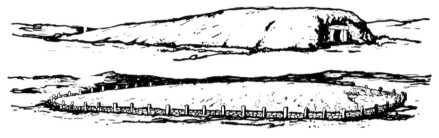

LATE NEOLITHIC LONG BARROWS OR BURIAL MOUNDS.

With little more than stone and flint tools, they began the clearance of trees on the uplands and other light soils. They mined flint after they found the nodules of fresh flint, bedded in layers in the chalk, was greatly superior to surface flint. After this, they developed such industries as pottery making, leather working, spinning and weaving.

They were skilled in the utilization of wool. Spindle whorls of stone, bone and clay, as well as wooden spindles, have been found on certain prehistoric sites. They may have also been skilled in knitting. Since flax was cultivated, there can be little doubt that comfortable undergarments were worn.

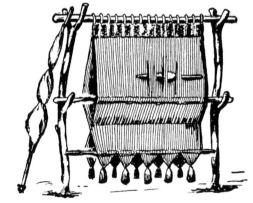

PRIMITIVE LOOM WITH WEIGHTS, DISTAFF AND SPINDLE.

16

Early homes were skin and felt tents, characteristic of the nomadic pastoral peoples of Europe and the steppes of Asia. More permanent homes arose through the preference for pit-dwellings. Such pits were merely circular holes about four feet deep and twelve feet in diameter. The excavated earth was piled around the pit to form a rampart. Their roofs were constructed of branches, thatched with reeds.

It is quite evident that the term "Stone Age" is inadequate in so far as it applies to the life style of these early inhabitants of Britain. Neither is it sufficient in dealing with artifacts, for some people made more use of horn and bone than stone.

TOOLS, IMPLEMENTS AND UTENSILS OF THE WINDMILL HILL PEOPLE.

The New Stone Age was giving way to the Bronze Age in most parts of the world when, around 2700 B.C., new groups of people known as the Secondary Neolithic People crossed France to southwest England, landing mainly near the shores of the Bristol Channel. These new arrivals continued the practice of building and burying their dead in massive stone encased tombs known as "Long Barrows", which were covered with extensive piles of earth. Some long barrows were as large as 50 feet wide and 300 feet long.

In some areas, megalithic tombs were constructed of large and often immense blocks of stones, forming passages or galleries, covered by long mounds as massive as the long barrows. The West Kennet Long Barrow is the largest and probably one of the earliest of these tombs in Britain. It measures 350 feet in length and contains five burial chambers.

WEST KENNET LONG BARROW

The burial practice involved lengthy and complex ceremonies. The dead were laid out one by one, at the time of death, until upwards of fifty individuals had been cared for. With each interment, food, tools, flint arrowheads and, occasionally, pottery were placed in the grave before it was sealed.

Apparently, these builders were soon absorbed by the earlier colonists. Most of the pottery and other artifacts found in their tombs have been of the earlier type.

TOOLS, WEAPONS AND POTTERY OF SECONDARY NEOLITHIC PEOPLE

We may attribute the technique of building with large stones to these Secondary Neolithic People. Later, this technique was to be copied (on an even larger scale) by other people at Avebury and Stonehenge. They were also skilled in working with wood, since it was they who built the roofed temples at the Sanctuary and Woodhenge and the large open air sanctuaries, of which Stonehenge is the finest and best known example.

Soon after 2300 B.C., new bands of immigrants from Holland and the Rhineland began to reach Britain. Known to the archaeologist as the Beaker People (from the occurrence of pottery drinking vessels in their graves) they soon established themselves masters over the native population. They seem to have been well organized and less peaceable than the Windmill culture, as evidenced by the large number of weapons found buried with their dead.

TYPICAL BEAKER VESSELS (a) BELL (b) SHORT-NECKED (c) LONG-NECKED

Following a practice of their predecessors, the Beaker people settled, for the most part, in those districts where they could procure a regular food supply; areas in which they obtained the raw materials for implements, weapons and trade goods. Therefore, the distribution of megalithic monuments in Britain is heaviest in those areas having mineralized geological formations. (see pg. 20)

The Beaker people departed from the older custom of collective burial and interred their dead singularly, or sometimes by twos, in small rounded graves marked by mounds. Sometimes, they made coffins of stone slabs. Although they were not so imposing as those of their predecessors, they were often more richly stocked with Bronze Age treasures, such as gold, amber and jet ornaments. After about 1500 B.C. the bodies were mostly cremated.

One of the main activities of the Beaker people was the development of metal trade. They sought out and opened up the main trade routes between the copper and gold mining areas of Ireland and their main settlements, along the eastern coast of Britain. The dominant position of the Beaker people was due, in part, to their possession of the earliest objects of metal (copper and gold) to have been found in Britain. Apparently, in those ancient times, Britain had its own trading colonies which were often visited by active and enterprising seafarers.

The Beaker people's ritual temples or "henges" are peculiar to Britain. They consist of one or more oval or circular ditches, with

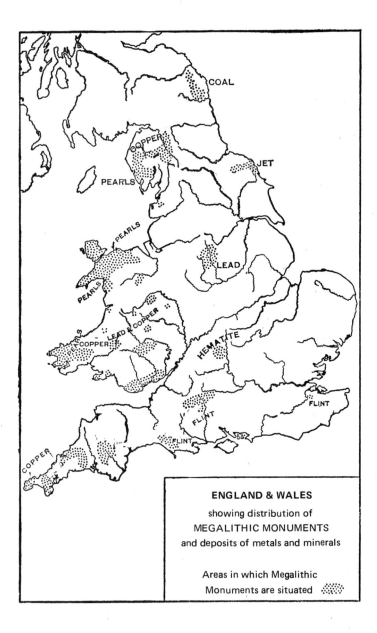

COAL

COPPER

JET

PEARLS

PEARLS

PEARLS

LEAD

PEARLS

LEAD & COPPER

COPPER

HEMATITE

FLINT

FLINT

FLINT

COPPER

ENGLAND & WALES

showing distribution of
MEGALITHIC MONUMENTS
and deposits of metals and minerals

Areas in which Megalithic
Monuments are situated

internal or external banks, ranging in diameter from a few yards to a quarter of a mile. Usually they have two or more entrances and a ring of stones, surrounding the internal or sacred space.

Other types of ritual monuments found dating from the same period are the alignments and avenues of free-standing upright stones, and ditch-and-bank earthworks. At Stonehenge, the Beaker people planned a double circle of "bluestone" (a special kind of igneous rock) uprights, with an elaborate entrance. They never completed it, although the stones were laboriously transported from the Prescelly Mountains of Pembrokeshire.

Following after the Beaker people, the "Wessex" people appeared on the Salisbury Plain around 1700 B.C. Some scholars give their origin as Brittany, France, citing similarities in cultures of that period; others favor Central Europe. One Scottish archaeologist, V. Gordon Childe, suggests they simply developed in Wessex.

In any event, they are known to have been highly organized and industrious people, less inclined to warfare, preferring trade and the enjoyment of good living. Their rulers were great chieftains who, in a few decades, established a commercial aristocracy having trade relations from as far as Central Europe and Scandinavia to the urban civilizations of Crete, Greece and Egypt.

The Wessex people, as did their predecessors in Ancient Britain, have long since vanished as distinct societies. Because of assimilating and being assimilated by continuing waves of migrations and conquests, our only record of them is the objects they left in the burial tombs of their chieftains and the enduring monuments of Salisbury Plain. The greatest of these is Stonehenge.

LOOKING SOUTH-WEST

LOOKING NORTH—WEST

22

HISTORY OF CONSTRUCTION

As the result of archaeological excavations and investigations, it is now concluded that the building of Stonehenge covered a span of about 1600 years: between 3000 and 1400 B.C.

PERIOD I (between 3000 −2000 B.C.)

The earliest structures were the great circular ditch and two banks, (one on each side of the ditch) the Heel Stone, the Aubrey Holes and possibly some central feature. The entrance gap left in the banks and ditch, at the northeast, was about 35 feet wide and near this entrance were dug the four small holes, that may have held wooden posts. The two larger holes nearby, are believed to have held upright stones, forming a kind of doorway.

A cluster of small post holes were dug within the causeway (crossing the ditch) where the Avenue enters the monument. These holes formed at least five rows running concentrically with the ditch and banks, and some eight rows arranged radially from the center of the circle of Aubrey Holes. These holes may have also held wooden posts.

Both banks are composed of the solid chalk, excavated from the ditch, which covers the surface of the Salisbury Plain. The outer bank, now nearly obliterated, formed a fairly true circle, some 380 feet in diameter, about 8 feet wide and 2 or 3 feet high. The inner bank, about 20 feet wide and at least 6 feet high, formed the rim of a circle some 320 feet in diameter.

Many antler picks, used to excavate the chalk blocks forming the two banks, were found in the chalk rubble left in the ditch. Also uncovered in the ditch were fragments of Beaker pottery, a few flint implements and fragments of hammer-stones. Other finds included various articles discarded by visitors from Roman times to the present day.

Some 100 feet outside the entrance gap there is a third stone, now know as the "Heel Stone." It is about 20 feet long and about 8 feet wide by 7 feet thick. Its lower 4 feet are buried in the ground. The stone is a kind of natural sandstone which occurs 20 miles north of Stonehenge. Unlike all the sarsen megaliths, erected in later periods, it is entirely natural, bearing no marks of being dressed by chipping or scraping. Circling the Heel Stone some 12 feet from its base there is a ditch, dug presumably, to indicate the stone's special significance.

Just within the inner bank, these early Stonehenge builders dug the ring of 56 Aubrey Holes, forming a quite accurately measured circle, 288 feet in diameter. The holes vary from 2½ to nearly 6 feet in width and from 2 to 4 feet in depth. Although irregular in shape, there is little irregularity in their spacing, averaging nearly 16 feet. Apparently, the holes were filled and dug up and refilled on more than one occasion. Mixed with chalk used to fill the holes was found wood ash, flint flakes and cremated human bones.

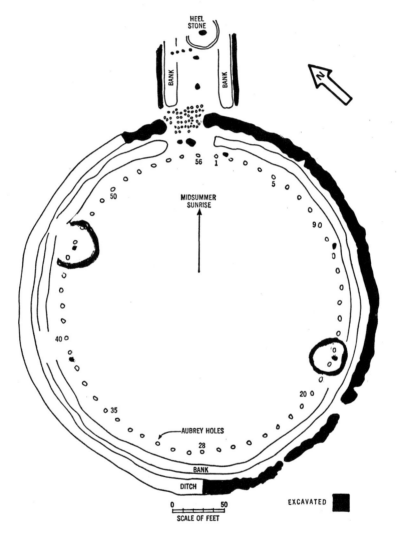

PLAN OF STONEHENGE I

A piece of charcoal excavated from the secondary filling of one hole, in 1950, gave a calibrated date of about 2200 B.C. (The method known as carbon 14 dating is based on the fact that every living thing, plant or animal, absorbs radioactivity throughout its life, and at death starts to lose it at a constant, measurable rate. The amount of carbon 14 it retains at any later time, as measured by geiger counters, thus indicates its age — as old as 30,000 years — plus or minus a margin for deviation. The diffculty with it is that such testable archaeological samples as charcoal and charred bones are not always "pure", as carbon 14 from more than one source may be disintegrating in them. As a result, the best age estimates of Stonehenge are still open to question). In any event, it has been suggested the circle of Aubrey Holes was dug some 200 years after the construction of the circular ditch and banks and were originally intended for wooden posts.

As the result of research carried out in California, on some very ancient trees called bristlecome pines, the whole system of radiocarbon datings has had to be revised. The conclusion has been drawn that all radiocarbon dates obtained from Bronze Age and Stone Age objects have been underestimated by several centuries. This would push the beginning of Stonehenge I back to about 2775 B.C. Until these dates are confirmed by some other scientific discoveries or datings processes they can only be accepted as a possibility.

Thus, we find at the end of the first stages in the development of Stonehenge: a simple but imposing circular "temple": a circular ditch with two banks, the larger inside the circle: three standing stones: four wooden posts and a ring of refilled holes. The whole, oriented in such manner, that a person standing in the center of the circle and looking toward the entrance, would see the sun, on midsummer mornings, just to the left of the heelstone.

It is believed that during or shortly after the first phase of Stonehenge building, the builders erected the four "station stones", approximately on the circle of Aubrey holes. They form a rectangle, perpendicular to the midsummer sunrise line of the monument. Only two of them remain. Originally, each stood on a so-called mound, bounded by a ditch. Both the remaining stones are sarsens, but very different in size and shape. One is a naturally shaped rough boulder about nine feet long, which now lies prone against the inner side of the old bank. The other is about four feet long and still stands upright. Its north and south sides have been slightly tooled.

LOOKING NORTH -EAST TOWARD THE HEEL STONE

BLUESTONES IN FOREGROUND

PERIOD II (between 2000 — 1700 B.C.)

The second phase of building added, but never completed, the double circle of bluestones and the Avenue. At least 82 bluestones, weighing up to 5 tons each, were set up in two concentric circles around the center of the enclosure. The double circles had a small entrance on the northeast side formed by a gap in the rings and marked by additional stones, on either side of the gap.

The old entrance gap in the ditch and bank was widened into the 40 foot wide "Avenue," bordered by a parallel ditch with banks on either side, some 47 feet apart. The Avenue was probably used as a road for hauling the bluestones from the river to the monument.

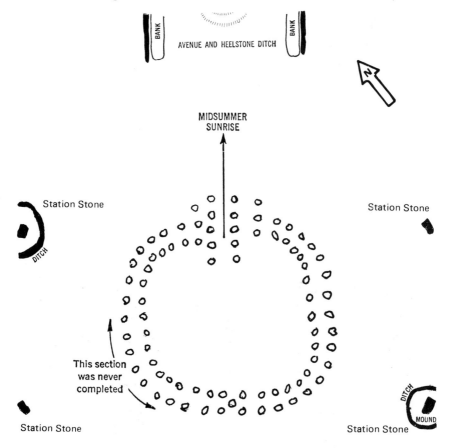

PLAN OF STONEHENGE II

Beginning about 1700 B.C. the final period of construction at Stonehenge began and with it the Bronze Age of Britain. This final phase of building was apparently done by a different group of people believed to be the Wessex People. Three distinct stages can be seen:

Stage III a: The double circle of bluestones, began in Period II and still incomplete, was removed and replaced by 81 or more huge sarsen stones, similar to the Heelstone in composition. These sarsen stones were placed in the same general area which the bluestones circles had occupied, but in a very different arrangement: a lintelled circle and the horseshoe outline of trilithons which we see today. A gateway was then formed by the Slaughter Stone and its missing companion, and the four Station Stones in the circumference ring of the Aubrey Holes were placed in position.

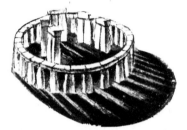

Stage III b: This phase of building may have been a continuation of the previous construction or it occurred shortly afterwards. Some 20 or more of the dismantled bluestones were carefully dressed to shape and re-erected in an oval design, within the Sarsen Horseshoe. Too few stone-holes for this setting have been indentified, to date, to ascertain the exact plan. At this time, the "Y" and "Z" holes were dug and it is believed they were to have been used to erect the remaining 60 bluestones, which had not been dressed to shape. For some unknown reason, this project was abandoned, unfinished, and the oval setting of dressed bluestones, in the center of the horseshoe, was removed.

The "Y" and "Z" holes form two irregular circles just outside the Sarsen Circle. No conclusive evidence has been found as to their use. They vary from 35 to 40 inches deep. Some of the excavated holes showed evidence of having been left open and allowed to fill naturally by the erosion of their sides (for some period of time) before being filled up completely. In some instances the partially filled holes were used as hearths; one contained early Iron Age pottery.

These last builders placed the great stones in such a manner so as to leave undisturbed most of the earlier stone alignments, even though those alignments were duplicated in their stones. The horseshoe of 5 huge trilithons, erected around the center of the monument opened to the northeast, so that its axis corresponded to the familiar mid-summer sunrise line of Stonehenge II.

Stage III c: The final reconstruction of Stonehenge, again probably a continuation of the previous work, saw the uprights of the dressed oval structure reset in a horseshoe of bluestones, a few feet inside the Sarsen Horseshoe. This is the pattern we see today. They also erected a circle of bluestones between the Sarsen Horseshoe and the Sarsen Circle. It also had its opening to the northeast, in keeping with the original design, but was otherwise quite irregular in shape.

The number of bluestones in their circle is difficult to calculate. Over half of them have been demolished and most of the remaining ones, leaning or broken. The estimated count ranges from 56 to 61, although 59, a number suggested by Dr. Gerald S. Hawkins (Boston University Professor and astronomer at the Smithsonian Astrophysical Observatory in Cambridge, Massachusetts) is the most acceptable. This happens to be the number of "Y" and "Z" holes dug, but never used.

When completed, Stonehenge stood unique in the refinements of its detail. Apart from the barrows, it is the only monument attributed to the Wessex culture. However, it is important to understand that Stonehenge cannot be regarded as a single identity as was believed at the beginning of this century. Rather, it is a monument recording the building abilities and scientific research of many generations of intelligent though apparently illiterate people. The progressive structural changes reveal to us their search for astronomical knowledge and understanding.

Planning such an undertaking, as Stonehenge, would suggest a concentration of political power, for a time at least, in the hands of one man, who could create and program the conditions necessary for such a project. In a society governed by chieftains, our builder had to possess adequate on-going influence in that he initiated plans which could not be completed in his lifetime. It is unlikely that such a remarkable personage would have gone unnoticed in historical accounts. Possibly we know him as a personality in other settings, under other circumstances.

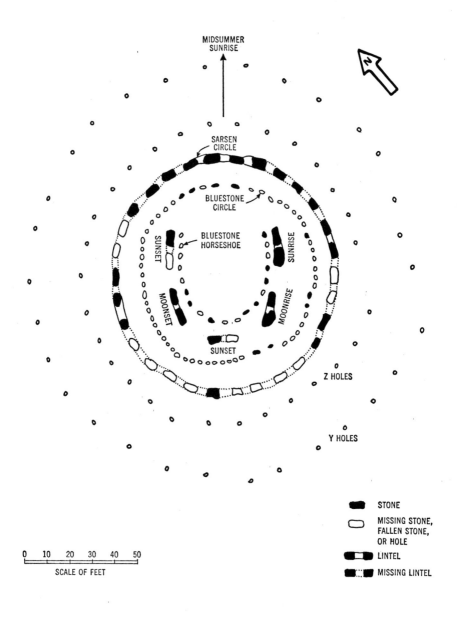

PLAN OF STONEHENGE III

SHOWING THE ORIGINAL POSITION OF THE STONES,

AND THOSE FALLEN OR MISSING

THE STONES

No one can look up at the huge megaliths on England's Salisbury Plain without wondering how a so-called primitive people with scant engineering knowledge could have brought them to the lonely spot and erected them. Yet, this mystery is not difficult to solve, for the job did not require miraculous powers or any startling ingenuity. In fact, actual demonstrations have shown how the ponderous blocks were conveyed from the quarries to the building site.

By means of petrological identifications, the source of the great bluestones has been located in the Prescelly Mountains (in north Pembrokeshire, Wales) some 130 miles distance from Stonehenge. Here, in an area of about one square mile at the eastern end of the mountains, is a "stone yard" of assorted stones (dolerite, rhyolite, ash and sandstones) deposited by ice during the Pleisocene period.

The so-called bluestones, selected by the builders of Stonehenge, are mainly the spotted dolerite, a blue-green stone with small whitish pink spots, varying in size from a quarter inch to one inch in diameter. The exception is the Altar Stone, which is a micaceous sandstone, which may have come from Milford Haven (Mill Bay) on the southwest coast of Wales.

There has been much speculation on just how and by what route these stones were transported to the Stonehenge site. Considering the alternative answers of a land or water route, the advantages of the waterway, in prehistoric times, is apparent. The finding of a very large number of objects, dating from Neolithic times onward, dredged in modern times from riverways, shows a prevailing use of water transport.

If it is accepted that the bluestones were transported by water, then the question follows, what type of craft was used? The alternatives are rafts, made of solid logs lashed together, or true boats, hollowed out of logs. Actual remains of such boats have been dredged from river beds. Three or more such boats, lashed together, could satisfactorily carry the Altar Stone and a crew of at least ten men.

For the sea journey, the raft has some marked advantages over the boat in that it is unsinkable and cannot be swamped in rough weather. Regardless of which of the water craft was used, part of the journey to Stonehenge would have had to be made overland. The most probable route, over which the stones could have traveled, was worked out by Professor R.J.C. Atkinson of the University College, Cardiff.

From the place where the stones were found and partially shaped, they were pulled on sleds which rolled over log rollers, laid crossways on a log road bed, down to Milford Haven, a small bay on the southwest coast of Wales. There they were loaded on rafts or boats, propelled by oars and sails.

The most likely sea route would have followed the southern coast of Wales, west, and up the Bristol Channel to Avonmouth, then up the Bristol Avon and Frome Rivers to near Frome, in Somerset. After being unloaded from the sea crafts they were carried overland to the Wylye River, down that stream to the Salisbury Avon River and thence to Amesbury and the Stonehenge Avenue. The total distance is about 240 miles.

The transportation of eight or more bluestones, weighing up to five tons each is a feat never before attempted by any other people anywhere else in prehistoric Europe.

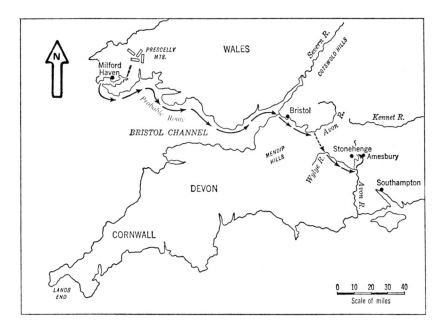

PROBABLE ROUTE OF THE BLUESTONES FROM THE PRESCELLY MOUNTAINS IN WALES TO STONEHENGE

In 1954, Professor Atkinson demonstrated the practicality of this route by re-enacting the transportation of the stones. He took a replica of a bluestone, made out of concrete, and lashed it to three "canoes" built of elm boarding and measuring 12' X 2'3" X 1'6".

34

These were fixed together by four transverse beams. The total load, including a crew of four, was about 3,600 pounds and gave a draught of 9 inches. The loaded boat was "poled" up and down a shallow stretch of the river Avon, with ease, showing the practicability of such a craft for the inland part of the voyage route from Prescelly. There is no record of such a test being conducted at sea. In the case of the sea route, the use of rafts is more likely the method of transport. Another suggestion for the water transport of the stones is that they were hung in the water between dug-out canoes or skin boats, which would be much safer than carrying the heavy stones in a boat.

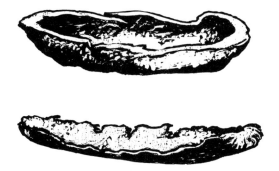

PRIMITIVE DUGOUT CANOES

The overland test consisted of taking the concrete replica of the bluestone and lashing it to a simple wooden sled. The loaded sled was then dragged over the down, immediately south of Stonehenge, by a party of 32 sturdy young schoolboys, arranged in ranks of four along a single hauling rope, each rank holding at chest level a wooden bar to whose center the rope was fastened. It was found that they could just pull a 3500 pound load up a slope of about 4 degrees (1 in 15), though it is doubtful whether they could have continued this effort for a long time. The sled slid easily over the long rank grass, and left no sign of its passage apart from some slight crushing.

When rollers were placed under the sled, using the house-mover's technique of continually taking the rollers from back to front as they came out from under, the total number of boys needed to move the stone was reduced to 24. Some of this number were occupied with the additional problem of steering. As the rollers were used when climbing a slope, obliquely, there was a natural tendency for the sled to slip sideways off the rollers. To counteract this, guide ropes were attached to the four corners of the sled, manned by two persons at each corner.

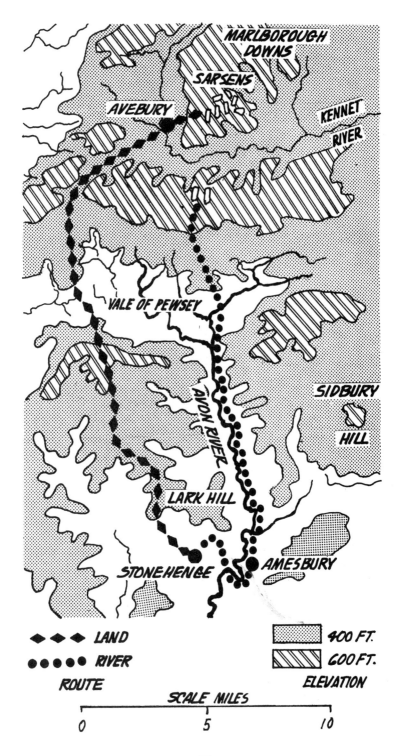

MARLBOROUGH DOWNS

SARSENS

AVEBURY

KENNET RIVER

VALE OF PEWSEY

AVON RIVER

SIDBURY HILL

LARK HILL

STONEHENGE

AMESBURY

◆ ◆ ◆ LAND

● ● ● ● ● ● RIVER

ROUTE

▨ 400 FT.

▩ 600 FT.

ELEVATION

SCALE MILES

0   5   10

The huge sarsen stones came to Stonehenge from Marlborough Downs, some 20 odd miles to the north. At the time, they must have been in such profusion that no quarrying was required. As late as 1747, John Wood wrote, "Marlborough Downs...are covered with vast quantities of stones of the very same kind as the light colored pillars of Stonehenge...scattered upon the surface of the earth."

Two areas have been suggested as the actual site from where the sarsen stones were selected. One site is just east of Avebury. From there, the generally accepted route of the stones' passage to Stonehenge was entirely over land. Another possible site is an outcrop, south of the Kennet River. From the latter site an alternate route has been proposed by Patrick Hill, geologist of Carleton University, Ottawa, which would utilize the Avon River over half of the distance. (see map pg. 36) Although the Avon is now only about two feet deep, Hill suggests climatic conditions could have been much different in those days, making the Avon much deeper. Another suggestion is, the Avon may have been dammed near Amesbury to add depth to the stream.

The method of transportation of the sarsen stones to Stonehenge site was, in all probability, the same as was used to convey the bluestones overland. The sarsen stones weigh from between 20 to 50 tons. This far greater weight would require both a closer setting of the rollers (in order to distribute the weight and prevent their being driven into the ground) and a larger diameter of the rollers, as well, to avoid breaking them when passing over irregularities on the surface.

Using the ratio of 16 men per ton, as estimated by the pulling of the bluestones, it would require between 320 and 800 men to pull such stones. An additional force of perhaps 200 more would be needed to clear brush and move the rollers, when needed.

If we allow an average rate of progress of half a mile per day, over the 24 miles to Stonehenge, it would take about 7 weeks for the journey and require some 1250 men, working continuously. Several rather steep slopes, to be encountered on the overland route, would require an additional working force of probably 250 men.

Since some time must be allowed for the returning journey from Stonehenge, presumably with the empty sleds and the rollers, and for the necessary rest and recuperation; it would be more realistic to allow 9 weeks for the round trip. On this basis, it can be calculated that the task would require 1500 men, working for over five and a half years, allowing for no major interruptions due to bad weather. However, it would not be unreasonable to assume that the transport of the sarsen stones took upwards of ten years.

MOVING THE SARSENS TO
STONEHENGE ON ROLLERS

HOW WAS IT BUILT?

From several scientific excavations in modern times, we can, by reasonable interpretation of tools and toolmarks (and by common sense) reconstruct the building procedure.

The earthworks, large and small, all seem to have been made with the simplest tools. The chalk was loosened with picks, (made from the antlers of red deer) probably sharpened and driven into the chalk, then pried up, to break the chalk in fragments. By rakes made from antlers, or small shovels made from the shoulder-blades of oxen, the loose chalk was raked or shoveled into baskets and carried to the bank and emptied. Several helpers (to carry the baskets of chalk) were probably assigned to each digger. As the ditch became deeper, they could have used ladders made of notched tree trunks.

The stone tools used in the construction of Stonehenge were of four kinds:
1. Flint axes of crude form, roughly chipped, with a cutting edge.
2. Flat hammer-axes chipped to an edge on one side and flat on the other.
3. Flint rounded hammer-stones, many of which showed signs of bruising and hard wear.
4. Sarsen rounded hammer-stones varying in weight from one pound to six and a half pounds. These were used for surface dressing of the stones.
5. Sarsen mauls weighing between twenty and sixty pounds. The broadest side of these were more or less flat and could be wielded by two or three men.

HAMMER STONE

The stones, used in the construction, were most likely split to approximately the required size and roughly shaped at the quarry site. Splitting could have been done by driving dry wooden wedges in natural cracks, which, when soaked with water, would swell. The resulting pressure would split the stone, along the crack. Another method could have been heat, applied to the stone by a line of fire, placed along a desired line of cleavage, followed by cold water poured suddenly on the heated surface. Where the cleavage line was subjected to the hot-to-cold stress, heavy stones or mauls, dropped along the line, would have opened the line to a crack.

When the natural or rough hewn boulders reached Stonehenge, the finished shaping and polishing began. For this purpose, stone mauls (naturally shaped boulders of sarsen) weighing as much as 60 pounds, were used. By pounding the surfaces with these mauls, the stones were reduced to an approximation of the desired final. For the final shaping, some stones appear to have had heavy sarsen stones pulled back and forth over them, using wet crushed flint as an abrasive.

Although only a few of the bluestones at Stonehenge were dressed, all the sarsens received some degree of dressing. The natural rough and pitted appearance they have today is the result of centuries of weathering which has not been uniform. Sarsen stone is not homogenous, that is, it varies in hardness from flint-like to soft sandstone easily crushed by hand. Therefore, wind and rain have hollowed deep holes in some of them. The slight grooves, to be seen in some lights, are the marks of continually pounding the stone in one direction. Much of the original finish of the stones has been lost through vandalism. In the 1800's, visitors to Stonehenge could rent hammers for the specific purpose of chipping off mementos.

The erection of the upright sarsens required holes being dug to specific depths to accommodate the variable lengths of the stones. This was necessary so that when erected, their tops were at the correct level. The holes approximate a rectangular shape, matching that of the stones, but are some 9 inches to a foot wider all around. Three sides of the holes are steep. The fourth side (toward the center of the site in the case of the trilithons, and away from it in the circle) is in the form of a ramp, sloping from the base of the hole proper to the surface, at an angle of about 45 degrees. Opposite the ramp, the hole was lined with a number of wooden stakes; their purpose being to protect the chalk side from being crushed by the toe of the stone as it was raised.

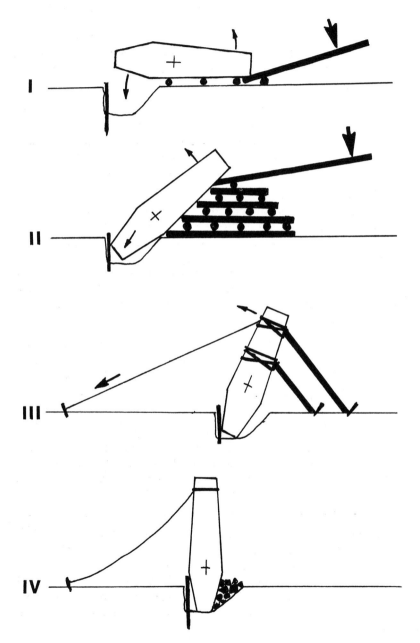

The stone to be raised was then aligned, radially, upon the stone hole and supported horizontally on rollers of large diameter, so as to raise it as far as possible above the surface. It was then dragged forward, still on a radial line, so that the front end, that is the base, began to overhang the ramp. When the center of gravity of the stone passed over the leading roller (which would be checked at this point by the stakes driven in the ground) it overbalanced, tipping the base squarely in the hole, leaving the lower part of the outer face resting on the ramp. In this way, the force of gravity alone would raise the stone about half-way to the upright position.

By attaching ropes to the top of the stone and pulling at the acute angle to the length of the stone (helped perhaps in the first stages by levers resting on timber cribbing) the stones would be pulled upright. The bases of all the uprights were left roughly pointed, on which the mass could pivot, so that a movement of a degree or two in any direction could easily be obtained.

When the final adjustment had been made, the space between the stone's base and the side of the hole was rapidly filled and rammed tight with stones and boulders. Many of these were discarded mauls, used in the previous surface dressing. When the hole and ramp had been filled and tightly packed with chalk rubble, the uprights were probably left for some time (some scholars suggest as long as a year) to allow for any settling before the work of fashioning uniform, level seatings for the lintels could begin.

It is probable that the lintels were being prepared during the interval when the uprights were left alone. It is likely the mortices were sunk, in the undersides, only after the work was resumed on the uprights and the tenons and dished seatings for the lintels completed. The necessary dimensions would have been transferred, by measurements, from one to the other.

In the outer circle of trilithons each upright had two tenons worked in its apex to bear the two lintels or horizontal stones which rested upon it. Corresponding mortices were sunk in these stones to admit the tenons. In the case of the trilithons of the inner horseshoe, only one tenon on each upright was necessary.

Evidently the stone masons found the cutting of the tenons a difficult task for the workmanship is not remarkable. By contrast the mortice holes were easier to cut and they are finished to a high degree of accuracy. This was probably accomplished by making a small depression in the stone, then filling it with sand and water. By inserting a round stone and continuously rotating it a smooth hollow could soon be worn.

FALLEN LINTEL SHOWING MORTICES

TRILITHON UPRIGHT SHOWING TENON

There is no direct evidence, at Stonehenge, to indicate exactly how the lintels were raised into position. Of several possible methods suggested, the most acceptable is one offered by Colonel R. H. Cunnington, in his "Stonehenge and its Date." (1935) His method employed the use of levers and the building of a timber "crib." This is a kind of tower, built of alternate layers of timbers, running in opposite directions. By levering one end at a time, (then placing temporary supports) additional layers of the crib would be laid around and beneath it; then planking laid on top to provide a working platform. This process would be repeated, over and over, till the lintels were just higher than the uprights; then they could be levered sideways into position and lowered over the tenons.

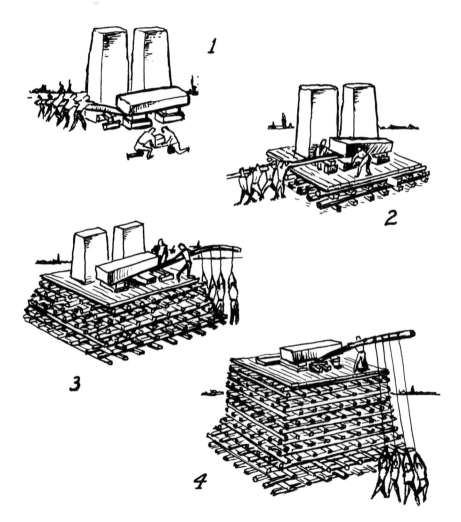

It is perhaps the lintels which set Stonehenge apart from all other megalithic structures in Britain. Not only are the lintels joined to the uprights by mortice-and-tenons, tongue-and-grooved to one another; they were also individually shaped to set in a particular place in the curve of the circle. The lintel stones, on the inner horseshoe setting, are wider at their tips than their bases to correct the apparent distortion produced by perspective.

LINTELS UPON UPRIGHTS

These features of construction suggest the builders were familiar with the techniques of carpentry as well as architecture. Such architectural refinement, at that time, could only be found in Egyptian and Middle Eastern civilizations, or the Grecian civilized centers of Mycenae and Crete.

This link with Greece was dramatically strengthened in 1953 when Professor R.J.C. Atkinson discovered a dagger carving on one of the sarsen stones. The shape of the dagger was unlike any of the British types, but was similar to daggers known to have been in use at Mycenae during the time when Stonehenge was under construction. One writer suggests the carving was the "architect's mark." Scores of other carvings of British bronze axe heads have been found on the sarsens.

Nowhere else in Britain or Europe can there be found the first stages of an architectural building comparable to Stonehenge. Therefore, it seems unlikely that the builders had arisen from the early megalithic builders of the so-called "Stone Age." (Neolithic and Beaker peoples)

ASTRONOMICAL DESIGN

For hundreds of years, archaeologists have probed around and under Stonehenge, in a vain attempt to understand what motivated its builders. Was it a sepulcher? A temple for pagan rites? Or a temple for sun worship?

In 1792, a man known today, only as "Warltire," suggested that Stonehenge has been a "...vast Theodolite (surveying instrument) for observing the motions of the heavenly bodies...erected at least seventeen thousand years ago." In 1829, one Godfrey Higgings stated that the arrangements of the stones represented "astronomical cycles of antiquity." He estimated its erection date to be about 4000 B.C.

In the 1800's other men noticed astronomical factors in the alignments of the uprights at Stonehenge. The most noted of these was Samuel P. Langley, founder of the Astrophysical Observatory of the Smithsonian Institute. Langley wrote, in 1889: "Most great national observatories, like Greenwich or Washington, are the perfected development of that kind of astronomy (astrophysics or positional observation) of which the builders of Stonehenge represent the infancy. These primitive men could know where the sun would rise on a certain day, and make their observation of its place."

Over 300 megalithic sites found in Britain were investigated and surveyed by Professor A. Thom (megalithic Sites in Britain — Oxford University Press — 1967) and found that what appeared to be crudest formed circles were actually complex geometrical figures resembling circles involving important astronomical alignments. Some of the circles were elongated, or egg-shaped, others flattened on one side and others ellipses. In all cases there was evidence that they had been laid out with great precision according to contemplated geometrical constructions. Professor Thom's analysis of the sight lines, given by the stone alignments, revealed the ability of the ancient builders to accurately predict eclipses of the moon. Furthermore, they could identify the small perturbation to which the moon's orbit is subject on account of the gravitational attraction of the sun.

Thanks to the admirable surveys of Sir William M.E. Flinders Petrie, Mr. Edgar Barclay, and Sir Norman Lockyer's precise azimuth alignments, the purpose of the circle is now known with certainty. Stonehenge was an ANCIENT OBSERVATORY!

The main axis of the monument was aligned to the midsummer sunrise. A man standing in the center and sighting directly over a 35 ton marker, would be looking directly to the spot on the northeast horizon where the sun rises at the summer soltice, the longest day of

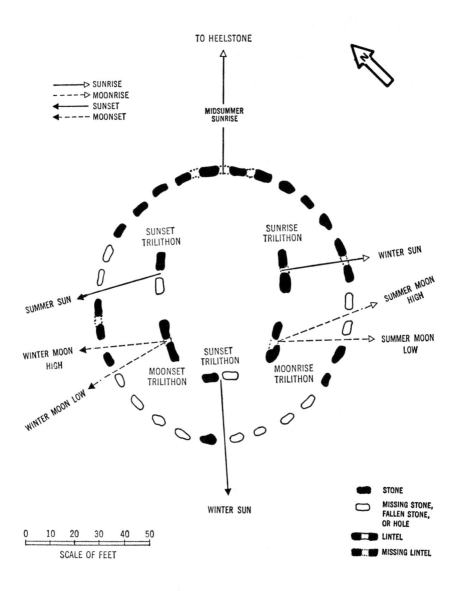

TO HEELSTONE

SUNRISE
MOONRISE
SUNSET
MOONSET

MIDSUMMER
SUNRISE

SUNSET
TRILITHON

SUNRISE
TRILITHON

WINTER SUN

SUMMER SUN

SUMMER MOON
HIGH

SUMMER MOON
LOW

WINTER MOON
HiGH

SUNSET
TRILITHON

WINTER MOON LOW

MOONSET
TRILITHON

MOONRISE
TRILITHON

STONE

MISSING STONE,
FALLEN STONE,
OR HOLE

LINTEL

MISSING LINTEL

WINTER SUN

0   10   20   30   40   50

SCALE OF FEET

CHART SHOWING ALIGNMENTS FOR THE ARCHWAYS

OF STONEHENGE PERIOD III

For complete and precise explanation, the reader is directed to
Dr. Gerald S. Hawkins' work "Stonehenge Decoded" (1965).

the year. The ancient builders had given themselves an accurate marker for midsummer day. From this special day every year, they could reckon forward to the times for plantings, harvests, hunting and other vital concerns for the whole year.

In visual observations, the sun appears to remain static or to repeatedly rise in the same position for several days at each solstice period. This makes it difficult to know the exact day of the solstice. However, the ancient builders marked a point of sunrise several days before the solstice day and then counted the number of days before the sun rise returned to the marked position. Half this number would mark the exact solstice day.

If the builders of Stonehenge had intended to simply mark the sunrise they needed no more than two stones. Yet scores of huge stones were carved and placed in position. Were there alignments to celestial bodies other than the sun, perhaps to the stars of planets or moon? Could Stonehenge be the "spherical temple" to the sun god, reported by Diodorus to have been on a northern island, where the people were careful observers of the moon and stars?

In 1965, Professor Gerald Hawkins, while standing in the center of the silent stones, was struck by the way the early architects had limited his exterior view. Looking through one of the narrow trilithons and an alignment archway in the outer ring, he wrote: "I felt that my field of observation was being tightly controlled, as by sighting instruments, so that I couldn't avoid seeing something." What the ancients were directing his attention to, Hawkins became convinced, was the rising and setting of celestial bodies, perhaps the sun or certain stars or planets. This was not a new idea. As far back as the 1700's, theories had been advanced as to other possible astronomical meanings at Stonehenge, but their wonderings had tended to be vague.

Hawkins, returning to the United States with accurate charts of Stonehenge, plotted the positions of its center point and of each significant stone, archway, hole and mound. Then he fed the data into a modern computer programmed to calculate the compass direc-

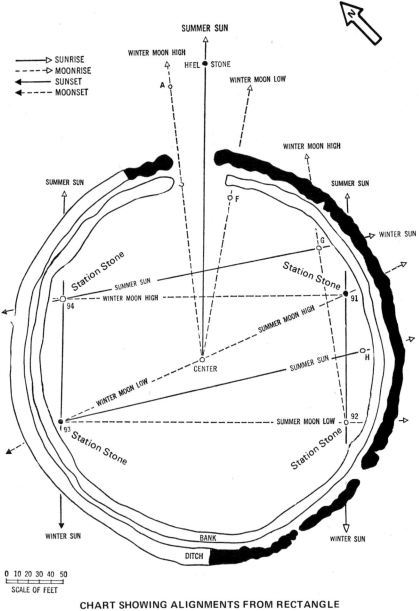

CHART SHOWING ALIGNMENTS FROM RECTANGLE
FORMED BY THE STATION STONES

For complete and precise explanation, the reader is directed to
Dr. Gerald S. Hawkins' work "Stonehenge Decoded" (1965).

tions established by 120 pairs of such positions and the points where a line drawn through them would meet the horizon.

The computer yielded some tantilizing results, and confirmed the earlier conclusions. Many of the Stonehenge alignments did accurately point to the summer and winter solstice positons of the rising and setting sun and moon — the extreme north and south latitudes reached only on midsummer day and on midwinter day, the shortest day of the year.

Thus the early Britons were able to determine, for instance, that winter started on the one day of the year when the rising sun was entirely visible just on the horizon through two carefully aligned arches. Additional plotting revealed that alignment of other stones had pinpointed equinoctial positions of the rising and setting sun and moon. This enabled Stonehenge observers to determine, accurately, the first day of both spring and fall. Concludes Hawkins: "Stonehenge was locked to the sun and moon as tightly as the tides. It was an astronomical observatory. And a good one, too."

Hawkins further suggests the 30 "Y" holes, the 29 "Z" holes and the Bluestone Circle of perhaps 59 holes could have served as day markers. "To predict the year of a possible eclipse would have been the most difficult task; Once the year was known, the month could have been noted by watching relative positions of sun and moon, a separate computer for counting days would have indeed been a useful luxury. Moving a stone around the bluestone circle each morning and evening would have marked an interval of 29½ days, a very fine fit to the lunar month." (Stonehenge Decoded — Hawkins)

The four "Station Stones" are believed to have been erected during the first part of the second phase of building. However, Hawkins suggests that they are actually a part of the first phase. The stones, numbered by the archaeologist, 91, 92, 93 and 94, standing approximately on the circle of Aubrey Holes, formed a rectangle perpendicular to the midsummer sunrise line of the monument. Only two of them, 91 and 93, remain.

Both the surviving stones are sarsens, but they are very different in size and shape. Number 91 is a naturally shaped rough stone, approximately 9 feet long, now lying in a fallen position against the inner side of the circular bank. Stone 93 is about 4 feet long and is still standing upright. Some tooling can be seen on its south and north sides. All four stones stood on so-called mounds, bounded by the customary ditch.

The short sides of the rectangle, formed by the Station Stones, parallel the direction of the center (Heel-Stone) axis; the long sides being almost exactly perpendicular to that axis. The diagonals of the rectangle intersected very close to the center of the Stonehenge I circle. This unique placement of the Station Stones, suggests they were immensely significant.

Three additional post holes found in 1966 (known today as the "Car Park Holes") were noted to serve as distance alignment markers when observed from the Station Stones and the Heel Stone positions. They pointed to sun and moon setting positions with extreme accuracy. Signs of decaying bark rings of tree trunks nearly two and a half feet in diameter were found in the holes. The height of such tree posts necessary to sight on the distant horizon, would have had to be some 30 feet tall.

An old artist's engraving of Stonehenge of around 1700 A.D. depicted two upright stones situated in a field toward the S.E. They are not there today. However, shallow depressions do exist in the area indicated by the drawing. In all probability, there are other post holes hidden under the turf awaiting discovery to add to our understanding of the remarkable astronomical achievements of the builders.

Scientists and scholars in our day have far too often assumed that little, if anything, was known in early days about true astronomical factors such as the actual length of the solar year. Yet, in Britain, we can find hundreds of ancient structural devices indicating the builders to have been in possession of similar astronomical knowledge.

In Scotland, Ireland and Brittany, in France, numerous complexes of standing stones are now acknowedged to have been oriented toward not only the summer and winter solstices and the equinoxes, but also toward the equivalent postitions of the moon. Like giant sundials, these stones marked the seasons rather than the hours.

Passage graves, centuries older than Stonehenge, have also been found to incorporate solar orientations. One of the most famous of these long, chambered passages, built of massive stones and covered with mounds of earth, is at Newgrange, Ireland. On Midwinter's Day the rising sun shines through a rectangular opening above the entrance and down the 70-foot long passage to illuminate the inner chamber in a deep, golden light. This impressive monument was constructed around 3250 B.C., several centuries before the earliest astronomical observations in the Near East, and even before the founding of the first Egyptian dynasty in about 3100 B.C.

Near the Oxford-Warwickshire border and near the towns of Chipping Norton and Long Compton are the Rollright Stones, sometimes called the "Little Stonehenge." It is a true circle of approximately seventy stones (the King's Men) with a diameter of 103.6 feet —

nearly the same as the Sarsen Stone circle of Stonehenge. A single menhir (the King Stone) is located several yards northeast of the circle. One quarter mile to the east lies the remains of a ruined dolmen, known as the "Whispering Knights."

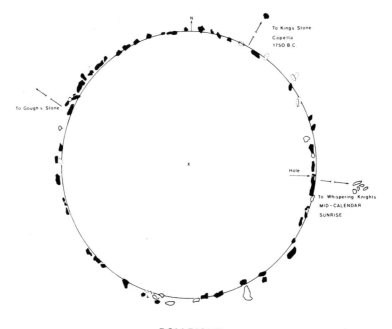

ROLLRIGHT

A stone on the east side of the circle has a hole bored through it. The Whispering Knights are visible through this hole as viewed from the center of the ring. Another stone with a hole, perhaps another intentionally indicated direction, is located on the north side of the circle. According to Professor Thom, some astronomical alignments are indicated by the relationship between the King's Men and the outlaying stones. The line from the center of the circle to the King Stone may indicate the rising point of the star Capella, in 1750 B.C. This date has been suggested as the date of Rollright's construction. Another line, to the east and through the Whispering Knights, indicates an astronomical declination that could have been used in a finely subdivided solar calendar.

ROLLRIGHT STONES (THE KING'S MEN)

THE KING STONE

AUBREY HOLES

One of the most puzzling mysteries of Stonehenge is the purpose of the 56 Aubrey Holes. It has always been obvious that they were; important. After being carefully spaced and deeply dug they were refilled. They never held stones or seemed useful as sighting points. Although they served as receptacles for cremated burials, sporadically; that use alone, would not give reason for so many holes, so evenly spaced. Their greatest radial error was 19 inches, and the greatest circumferential or interval-spacing error was 21 inches. Such accurate spacing of 56 points around the circumference of a circle of 288 feet in diameter was a remarkable feat of engineering.

It was not till Professor Hawkins was making his investigation of Stonehenge that the possible use of the Aubrey Holes was found. His solution suggests Stonehenge astronomy was so advanced that its experts had apparently noted a phenomenon, undetected even by modern astronomers: eclipses of the moon occurring in cycles of 56 years. Hawkins, who inadvertently rediscovered the cycle after running Stonehenge eclipse data through a computer, immediately associated it with the mysterious 56 Aubrey Holes that ring the massive arches. He concluded that the holes formed a primitive eclipse computer. By placing a stone in each of six appropriate holes and moving them at appropriate times one hole around the circle, he decided, the Stonehenge astronomers had probably been able to tell, accurately, the dates when solar and lunar eclipses were apt to take place.

From all this, Hawkins suggests that Stonehenge was the calendar by which the early Britons planted and harvested their crops, a shrine where they worshipped their gods and buried their dead, and a device that priest-rulers could have used to enhance their power. Although not a proven fact, he goes on to postulate that on the day or night that their stone computer predicted an eclipse, they might well have summoned their subjects to Salisbury Plain to observe a spectacle that would have terrorized most ancient people.

This is all very interesting but highly improbable. If Stonehenge had been built by some early "savages" who struggled to erect massive stones upright in the ground for some pagan, sacramental worship rites, then this might well have been the case. But in the light of our knowledge that Stonehenge was built with painstaking care (requiring a lengthy pre-planning period, both for architectural and organizational work requiring an advanced understanding of geometry and astronomy) it is evident that it was not constructed by "savages" but by educated and experienced engineers who lived in an intelligent, well organized, society.

THE SACRED CUBIT AND THE ROYAL CUBIT

Their interrelation as revealed by the Great Pyramid

$$1 \text{ Sacred Cubit} = \frac{10^3 \sqrt{\pi}}{4y} \text{ Royal Cubits} = 1.2132 \text{ Royal Cubits}$$

$$= 25 \quad \text{Pyramid inches} = 25.0265 \text{ Briitish inches.}$$

$$1 \text{ Royal Cubit} = \frac{4y}{10^3 \sqrt{\pi}} \text{ Sacred Cubits} = 0.82426 \text{ Sacred Cubits}$$

$$= 20.60659 \text{ Pyramid inches} = 20.6284 \text{ British inches.}$$

BOOK I — Elements of Pyramidology

One of the most important discoveries to come out of the study of Stonehenge is the fact that "Megalithic Man" possessed a standard unit of length. This is a tool so important that by itself it proves that the megalithic builders were quite different from the original picture of primitive farmers. The possession of a standard unit of measurement together with a standard unit of weight are the basis of architecture, engineering and other fundamental arts on which civilizations are built.

The standard unit of measurement found by Professor Thom, as the result of his survey of hundreds of stone monuments all over Britain, is defined as 2.72 British feet (32.62 British inches) and called the "Megalithic Yard." He concluded that standard Megalithic Yard rods must have came from a central headquarters, because if each small community had obtained the measure by copying the rod of its neighbor the accumulated error would certainly have exceeded 1.03 inches, and an error of even this magnitude would have been easily noted in his surveys. No noticeable differences were detected between the different sites.

Stonehenge, however, is unique in that the builders used the Egyptian Royal Cubit (20.6285 British inches) in its construction and the Megalithic Yard elsewhere. The Royal Cubit was used in the building of the Great Pyramid although a different unit of measurement, known as the "Sacred Cubit" (25.0265 British inches), was used in the design. Both the Megalithic Yard and the Royal Cubit bear a geometrical relationship to the Pyramid Sacred Cubit. The Sacred Cubit is revealed in the Great Pyramid as being subdivided into 25 equal parts, the subdivision being the "thumb-breadth," now known as the "Pyramid Inch." (1.001064 British inches)

The relationship between the two different Cubits can be readily seen in the high central section of the King's Chamber Passage, known as the "Ante-Chamber." (see diagram pg. 56) The length of the "Ante-Chamber" is equal to the diameter of the "Year Circle," a circle having a circumference of 365.242 Pyramid inches. This Year Circle is converted into a square of precisely equal area; the granite portion of the floor constituting the base of the square and the end of the granite East Wainscot forming the south side of the square. This means to say that the granite floor and the height of the said wainscot each defines the side-length of the square. The sides of this square are each found to measure exactly 5 Egyptian Royal Cubits of 20.6285 British inches or 20.6066 Pyramid inches. (more precisely 20.60659)

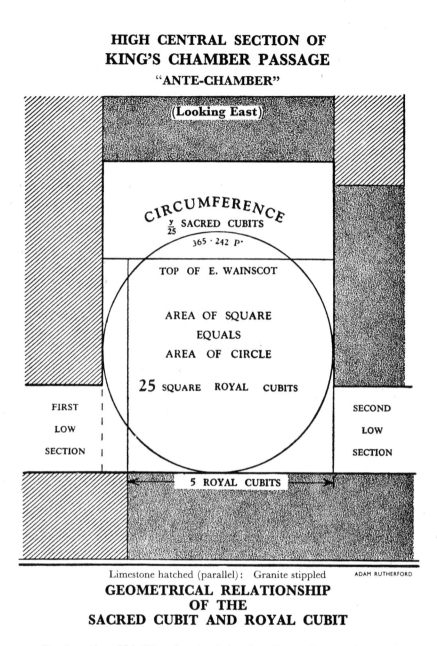

(Looking East)

CIRCUMFERENCE
$\frac{y}{25}$ SACRED CUBITS
365 · 242 P·

TOP OF E. WAINSCOT

AREA OF SQUARE
EQUALS
AREA OF CIRCLE

25 SQUARE ROYAL CUBITS

FIRST
LOW
SECTION

SECOND
LOW
SECTION

5 ROYAL CUBITS

Limestone hatched (parallel): Granite stippled   ADAM RUTHERFORD

**GEOMETRICAL RELATIONSHIP
OF THE
SACRED CUBIT AND ROYAL CUBIT**

During the Old Kingdom, when the Great Pyramid was built, the Royal Cubit was originally subdivided into 100 n. (1 n — 0.206285 of a British inch). The division of this cubit into 7 palms or 28 digits (4 digits to the palm) was a subsequent development. (See Encyclopaedia Britannica — 1956 — article "Measures and Weights.")

TRACING THE BUILDERS

The waymarks of the megalithic builders can be traced by the remains of their monuments (circles and mounds) forming a westward trail, between 3000 and 4000 years old. Beginning in the district north of the Persian Gulf, the route is found both north and south of the Mediterranean Sea to the coasts of Western Europe. From Portuagal and the Bay of Biscay in Brittany the trail separates, one going into Denmark, Sweden and Norway.

These stone structures can be roughly divided into three classes:
1. Menhirs (Celtic — "high stone") — Single upright stones which may be commemorative of some great event or personage.
2. Dolmens (Celtic — "table stone") — A stone slab set table-wise on three or more uprights.
3. Cromlechs (Celtic "stone circle") — A circle of stones sometimes enclosing barrows (tombs) or dolmens. Stonehenge is a highly specialized example of this last class.

NEAR HESHBON

NEAR HESHBON

ON MT. GILBOA

TRANS-JORDANIA

IN GALILEE

WEST OF HESHBON

ALGERIA

SPAIN

PORTUGAL

HAROLDSTOWN, IRELAND

MAIDSTONE, ENGLAND

ANGLESEY, WALES

The marked similarity of the chain of stone structures gives ample reason to believe that these time-defying monuments were erected by one race of people: the Hebrew people of the Old Testament. Some of the greatest fields of megalithic structures are to be found in the lands of ancient Israel, Central Asia and especially Trans-Jordanian territory. Menhirs, Stone Circles, Dolmens, Cairns, Mounds — all appear to have been constructed by the Hebrews, in Patriarchal times. The Bible makes frequent reference to the prominence of ''stones'' in the ritual and symbology of the ancient Hebrew people.

In Genesis, we read of Jacob taking the "stone" he had used as a pillow, setting it up as a "pillar" and "annointing" it. He called that place "Bethel," which means "God's House." (Gen. 28:18,22) Later, on the occasion of his covenant with Laban, " *Jacob took a stone, and set it up for a pillar. And Jacob said unto his brethren, Gather stones;*

and they took stones, and made an heap; and they did eat there upon the heap." (Gen. 31:45,46) Here, we see that Jacob constructed two of the most common types of ancient monuments: the single standing stone of witness, and the cairn, or collection of single stones by a multitude of witnesses.

Genesis 35, vs. 7 and 14 record where Jacob raised up other stone monuments in the form of an altar to "the God of Bethel", and a "pillar" of witness upon which he poured a drink offering. Moses is recorded, in Exodus, as rising early in the morning and building "*...an altar under the hill, and twelve pillars, according to the twelve tribes of Israel.*" (Exod. 24:4) There he assembled the people.

The Mosaic law provided for the construction of unhewn stone altars (Exod. 20:25; Deut. 27:5) and many examples of these can be found in the Holy Land. Israel was instructed to erect a pylon of "great stones" and to "plaister them with plaister" and to engrave the law thereon, in Mount Ebal. (Deut. 27:1-4) On Israel's crossing the Jordan, Joshua ordered the construction of a 12 stone cairn, or circle. (Josh. 4:3) Joshua later set up a "great stone" to serve as a witness to the covenant that Israel had made to serve the Lord. (Josh. 24:26-27)

Samuel set up a stone of witness called "Ebenezer "near Mizpeh. (I Sam. 7:12) Absalom set up a pillar of witness, and was later buried under a cairn. (II Sam. 18:17-18) It is most noteworthy that Jeremiah's instruction to scattered Israel (so-called Lost Tribes of Israel) was to "Set...up waymarks, make...high heaps" (Jer. 31:21) in the course of her migrations. This seems to have been an instruction to continue an already long established custom. Stone monuments and cairns, dating from the period of the migrations of Israel (700 B.C. to 500 A.D.), have been found along their routes through Scythia and Central Europe and on West.

These signs, when taken in conjunction with other remarkable links, afford convincing proof that the original colonists to Britain came from Accad, or Accadia. This was the Southern Province of Babylonia, the fertile district watered by the Tigris and Euphrates Rivers. In this country of the ancient Chaldees, the descendants of Shem, who was the father of the children of Heber (Ibiri, Abiri, or Hebrews), settled after the Flood.

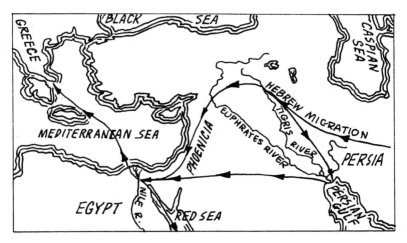

ANCIENT HEBREW MIGRATIONS

It should be noted that there is evidence which indicates that enterprising adventurers of the parent body of the Adamic Race (as distinct from the much earlier races) continued to leave their original Central Asia home. These migrations continued throughout the hundreds of centuries that preceded the Flood. (3145 B.C. — Bible Chronology — Dr. Adam Rutherford) They established colonies in various parts of the earth. These earlier settlers, in Babylonia and Egypt, introduced organized culture into the Tigris, Euphrates and Nile river valleys.

In discussing the Flood, it should be pointed out that although it is not commonly taught, there is ample proof that the Flood was NOT world-wide. When it says in the Scriptures that the Flood covered "the earth," the Hebrew word, used in the original writing by Moses, was "eh-rets," meaning "the land," or the particular area where it occurred. That is, it was a local flood which covered one particular region or land, not the whole earth.

The Chaldean civilization with its advanced mathematics and astronomy together with the scientific achievements of the Egyptians, during their Pyramid Age, has always baffled the archaeologists. This phenomenon can only be explained as resulting from an influx of people from the Semitic branch of the family of Noah, after the Flood.

This would also explain the famous astrology of the Chaldeans. The word "astrology" is, in fact, synonymous with wisdom. The early Chaldean priests were genuine astronomers. They knew the accurate value of the Solar year, divided the day into 24 hours, and the circle into 360 degrees. Their months consisted of 30 days each. They were able to calculate eclipses, compiling long lists of them. They discovered that the sun was "spotted," and recognized comets.

They knew the 12 signs of the Zodiac and from its constellations developed their famous "Astrology." The existence of certain values connected with the Procession of the Equinoxes, found in their records, indicate they had rules and methods of calculation, but did not know the principles that formed the basis of their calculations. This would suggest they had inherited their astronomy from the earlier Adamites.

The writings of Josephus, the historian, make reference to the Adamic origin of astronomy and mathematics: "They (the Sethites) also were the inventors of that peculiar sort of wisdom which is concerned with the heavenly bodies and their order." Ancient Persian and Arabian traditions also ascribe the invention of astronomy to Adam, Seth, and Enoch.

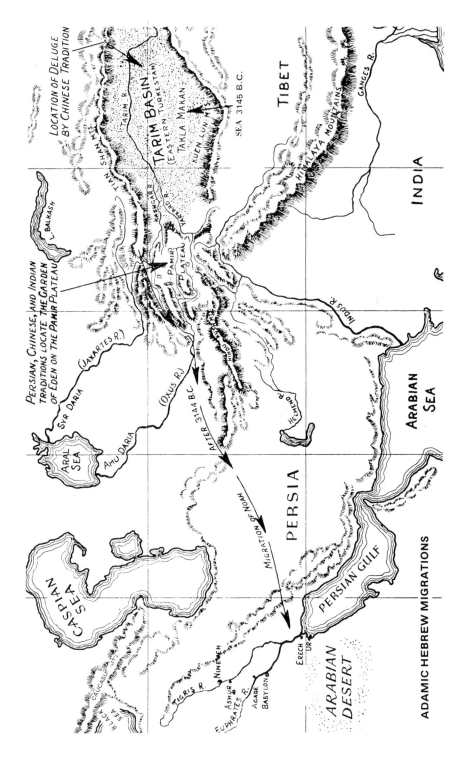

LOCATION OF DELUGE BY CHINESE TRADITION

TARIM BASIN (EASTERN TURKESTAN)

TAKLA MAKAN

TIEN SHAN MTS.

TARIM R.

KASHGAR R.

YARKAND R.

KUEN LUN M.

SEA 3145 B.C.

TIBET

GANGES R.

HIMALAYA MOUNTAINS

INDIA

PERSIAN, CHINESE, AND INDIAN TRADITIONS LOCATE THE GARDEN OF EDEN ON THE PAMIR PLATEAU

L. BALKASH

PAMIR PLATEAU

(JAXARTES R.)

SYR DARIA

AMU DARIA

(OXUS R.)

AFTER 3144 B.C.

HELMEND R.

INDUS R.

ARABIAN SEA

ARAL SEA

CASPIAN SEA

MIGRATION OF NOAH

PERSIA

PERSIAN GULF

ARABIAN DESERT

BLACK SEA

CAUCASUS MT.

TIGRIS R.

ASHUR

NINEVEH

EUPHRATES R.

AGADE

BABYLON

ERECH

UR

ADAMIC HEBREW MIGRATIONS

64

The Book of Jubilees is one of the non-canonical books of the Bible; yet it contains valuable information concerning the first 4000 years of Adamic history, ending about the time of the Exodus of the Hebrew people from Egypt. In the fourth chapter, we read of Enoch: "He was the first one among the children of men that are born on the earth to learn writing and knowledge and wisdom. And he wrote the signs of heaven according to the order of their months in a book, that the sons of men might know the time of the year according to separate months...and made known to them the days of the year and arranged the months and explained the sabbaths of the years as we made them known to him....."

One branch of the Adamic family developed from Eber, through Peleg and Abram of Ur, in the Chaldees. The name "Eber" or "Heber" means "colonizer" in the Hebrew-Phoenician language and history confirms that his descendants, the Hebrew-Phoenicians, have been the greatest colonizers and mariners in the world. From Chaldea they migrated to Phoenicia on the Mediterranean coast, from where they spread out on both sides of the Mediterranean.

Abram, whose name was changed to Abraham, was chosen of God to become the father of the Chosen or "Covenant People." (Gen. 17:4,5) He was also the father of three different divisions of the Phoenician-Hebrew people. Through Hagar, the bond maiden, he became the father of the Ishmaelites, the Arabs, many of them living today in India. But, only through Sarah, his rightful wife, did he become the father of the "Children of Promise" as the Apostle Paul wrote of them.

During the thousand years between Abraham and Solomon, the Hebrew-Phoenicians separated into widely divergent cultures, as they spread themselves among the aborigine. The descendants of Abraham grew into the mighty United Kingdom of Israel. (This included all 13 tribes of Israel in contrast to the descendants of the tribe of Judah, some of whom are part of the modern nation of Israeli). Other groups migrated west, across Europe and Africa, to Western Europe and the Isles in the West, marking their trails with the megalithic monuments that still exist to this day. Those that remained in Phoenicia established the commercial empire that became the undisputed master of the eastern Mediterranean.

As ship builders and navigators, as miners and metallurgists, as merchants and colonizers, they built trading centers and garrisons as far as Britain and the coasts of the North Sea. They manufactured articles of glass and metal, various types of weapons and jewelry, and they traded in grain, wine and cloth. It is believed they were the original manufacturers of the famed purple dyestuff which was extracted from the gland of the murex, or purple sea snail. They also imported science and the art of writing from Egypt, Crete and the Near East and spread it into Greece, Africa, Italy and Spain.

PHOENICIAN TRADE ROUTES

In the process of introducing, to many countries, their technical and artistic achievements they seemingly accepted the pagan religious practices of the people with whom they came in contact: the Baal worship of the Canaanites: Ishtar, the goddess of fertility, worshipped by the Babylonians and even child sacrifice to the god Moloch. In 204 B.C. the Carthaginians, also of Phoenician-Hebrew origin, offered 100 boys of noble birth on Moloch's fiery altars, in a vain effort to propitiate Moloch and raise the seige.

PHOENICIAN MERCHANT GALLEY

Historians, recording the activities of the Phoenicians, seem to have generally overlooked the fact of their kinship with, not only the early Britons, but also the Greeks and Trojans. The latter originally started as colonies of Hebrew peoples from Egypt, before the Exodus. (1453 B.C.)

In the history of the "Golden Age of Phoenicia," the term "Phoenician" was applied to only those hardy mariners, who sailed from the eastern shores of the Mediterranean, and to the inhabitants of the coastal land of Phoenicia. In world history they are noted for their unscrupulous dealings and piracy, which gained for them the reputation of "rogues." However, they were master craftsmen, in stone, metal and wood; talents that were employed by King Solomon, for the building of his temple.

All evidence indicates that people from the divergent Phoenicia — Hebrew colonies, migrating to Britain, became known to modern historians as the "Neolithic" people; the early inhabitants of Britain. Later waves of immigrant kinsfolk, following the trail blazed by the earlier Hebrew colonists, became the later Windmill and Beaker people. Coming by way of Africa, Spain, Greece and Crete, the latter, fusing with the first arrivals, probably formed the Wessex People. The individual groups vary in type so that it is not possible to speak of a "Megalithic People," but only of a megalithic "culture" and a social structure imposed upon the natives, among whom they came.

The brilliant British astronomer Sir Norman Lockyer, writes in his "Stonehenge and Other British Stone Monuments Astronomically Considered": "By the best light I can obtain, I judge our Tyrian Hercules made his expedition into the ocean, about the latter end of Abraham's time; and most likely 'tis, that Avebury was the first great temple of Britain, and made by the first Phoenician colony that came hither, and they made it in this very place on account of the stones of the gray-weather, so commodious for their purpose."

Professor L.A. Waddell, in his works, "Phoenician Origin of the Britons, Scots and Anglo-Saxons," provides convincing evidence gathered from hundreds of Phoenician coins and inscriptions. These coins (found in Britain and the East) seem to indicate the early Britons were the same sea-going Aryan-Phoenicians whose astronomer priests built devices with which they might study the heavens.

Another point that should not be overlooked is the similarity between British and Egyptian architecture, including the use of the Royal Egyptian Cubit. As long ago as 1913, Sir Grafton Elliot Smith (an Australian anthropologist) wrote a paper in which he ascribes the origin of the megalithic chambered tombs of Britain to the mastabas built in Egypt in the early part of the third millennium B.C.. Sir Mortimer Wheeler (Professor of entomology at Harvard University) also noted: "the general analogy between mastabas and many types of chambered tomb is too close to be altogether accidental."

Many remarkable similarities between alignments of the ancient stone "waymarks," in the east and the west, can be found. One such example is Avebury, one of the most ancient and by far the largest of the stone circles in Britain. It consists of two separate circles having diameters 325 feet and 350 feet, respectively, within a larger circle of 1260 feet in diameter. The circles were composed of large unhewn sarsens, weighing from 70 to 80 tons each. Only a few are left today, but an earthwall of 44 feet in height and one mile in circumference still exists. The only other circle in the world to compare with it, in size and construction, is the one near Darab, in Persia.

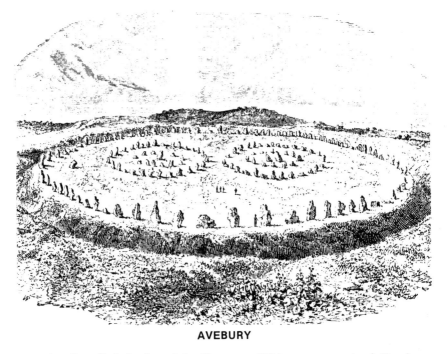

AVEBURY

Another link is found in the megalithic monument of Do-ring, (which means "The Lone Stone") in the highlands of Tibet, in Central Asia. Professor G.N. Roerich, in his "Trails to Inmost Asia," tells us they go back to pre-Buddhistic period of Tibetan history and "...consist of important alignments of 18 rows of erect stone slabs. Each of these alignments was drawn from east to west, having at its western extremity a cromlech, or stone circle, consisting of several menhirs arranged more or less in a circle."

The menhirs are vertically planted with a crude stone table, or altar, in front of them. It was evidently a sanctuary for some primitive cult. But what of its age and use? If one compares the famous megalithic monuments of Carnac, in Brittany, to the discovered megaliths of Tibet, he is at once struck by the remarkable similarity of the two sets of monuments. The Carnac alignments are situated from east to west and have at their western extremity a cromlech, or circle, of stones. The Do-ring monuments have precisely the same arrangement."

An interesting link was provided by the "Palestine Exploration Report on Sinai Peninsula" of 1873. They reported the discoveries of numerous "nawamis" (from namus, a mosquito house — the tradition being that the children of Israel built them as a protection against mosquitos) that exactly resembled the "bothan" (shielings) of the Shetland Islands and Clava, near Inverness, in Scotland. They were circular houses about ten feet in diameter, built of unhewn stone, and covered with a carefully constructed dome-shaped roof, the top of which is closed by a large slab of stone. The sides were weighted with stone, to prevent them from bulging out. The entrance was a low door, two feet high.

Sir Henry Morton Stanley, the famous British explorer, describes a circle of stones on the summit of Mt. Gerizim: "the Mount of God". He terms this the oldest Sanctuary in Palestine, and states it is nearly identical with the so-called Druidic circles of Britain. It was from such a circle, on Mt. Gerizim, that Melchizedek, the "Priest of the Most High God", came forth to meet Abraham, bearing bread and wine. From there he blessed Abraham and uttered the wonderful promises that have been so literally fulfilled.

The conclusion that can be drawn from all the evidence is that the early Britains who erected Stonehenge and other great megalithic monuments were either Hebrews themselves or progenitors of the Hebrews. They were the "Building Race" of the Bible, fathered by Shem. They built the Great Pyramid in Egypt. Down through the ages, groups of these people were continually moving westward, coming finally into the British Isles. They brought with them the knowledge, ability and acumen that enabled them to build Stonehenge.

A BRITISH DRUID
DRAWING BY WILLIAM STUKELEY, 1723

DRUIDISM

A writer of antiquity once wrote, "The history of a nation is the history of its religion, its attempts to seek after and serve its God." It is noteworthy that in Ancient Babylon, Persia and Asia, few ruins of palaces or dwelling are found. Mostly, we find magnificent remains of Temples; they witness to the importance the people of these countries attached to their religious worship. This has always been true of Great Britain, where the standing stone monuments from Orkney in the north, to Cornwall, in the south, witness to the vigour and vitality of its national religion — Druidism — one of the oldest religions in the world.

Under Druidism, Britain developed a high standard of religion, justice and a code of moral teaching that influenced her national character. On the principal, "the truth against the world," (Y Gwir Yn Erbyn Byb) dedicated priests built up a highly organized religious institution that wielded authority over the people of other nations. This priesthood established a system of national colleges under the supreme authority of Archdruids; who became Philosophers of renown to the outside world.

Although many modern historians accept that Druidism was the religion of Ancient Britain; they consider it unlikely that there were any "Druids" in Britain until many centuries after Stonehenge was built. The accepted theory is that the Druids were a Celtic priesthood which flourished in Britain, beginning a few centuries before the Roman Conquest.

Much confusion is avoided if we distinguish between the origin of the Druids and the origin of Druidism. The official order seems most likely to have originated in Celtic Gaul, while Druidism is pre-Celtic. It was adopted, with little modification, by the Celts, migrating into the British Isles. Although "Druids" did not actually erect the stone circles, such as Stonehenge; it is acceptable to believe that they played an important part in the whole concept of Stonehenge.

The origin of "Druid," is not known with certainty. One orthodox suggestion takes "uid" as meaning "knowing" and "dru" as a strengthening prefix, impling a very learned man (Encyl. Britannica). Another suggestion is that the name "Druid" is derived from "Druithin," meaning, "a servant of Truth."

In the year 1885 Professor Donald Mackinnon of Celtic Languages, Edinburgh University, offered the explanation that "Druid" is connected with and derived from the root that gives "drus" and "dendron" as meaning "oak" and "tree" respectively in the Greek;

71

"drus" as meaning "wood" in Sanskrit; "tree" in English; "doire" as "a grove," and "darach" an "oak," in Gaelic. Thus, in Mackinnon's opinion, the word "Druid" is derived from the word for an oak, although he added that after the fall of Druidism there is no question that the word "Druid" took on the meaning of a "wise man."

This thought is also expressed by E.O. Gordon in his works, "Prehistoric London"; "The title 'Druid' in Welsh, 'Der wydd' is said to be a compound of 'dar,' superior, and 'gywdd,' priest or inspector. The Irish 'Der,' a Druid, is the absolver and remitter of sins. The same root is found in the Persian 'duree,' a good and holy man, and in Arabic 'dere,' a wise man."

The Latin equivalent for Druids is "Magi" and was used by early Irish and Welsh writers. The term "Magi" may imply a kinship to the Magi of the New Testament record who saw "his star in the east" and came to worship the Christ Child.

It is acknowledged that most of our present day source material, relating to the Druids, is scanty and in the form of written documents, frequently in second-hand quotations. Greek and Roman writers make occasional references to Druids in describing the Celts and their religion. The earliest reference appeared around the beginning of the second century B.C. Then came the Irish folk-stories and hero-tales of the fourth and fifth centuries A.D. The later Irish and Welsh Triads provide a somewhat more revealing word picture of the Druids.

Julius Caesar wrote of the Druids: "They taught of the stars and their motions, the magnitude of the countries, the nature of things, and the power of God." Caesar further says of the Druids: "They hold aloof from war and do not pay war taxes; they are excused from military service and exempt from liabilities. Tempted by these great many young men assemble of their own motion to receive their training."

Archaeology has shed considerable light on the Celtic Culture (both in Europe and Britain); their building techniques, their weapons and tool types, their craftsmanship and burial modes. But, material directly related to Druids is still lacking. As far as it is known, no authentic pre-Roman inscription, referring to the word "Druid," has been found. In considering the archaeological evidence that may be related to the Druids, we find ourselves involved in assumptions and speculation.

In describing the attire of the various Druidic Orders, it must be pointed out that most of our information comes from the often highly imaginative and speculative writings and illustrations of 16th and 17th century writers. This was a period which began with a revival of interest in the Druids and culminated, in the Late Victorian period, by presenting the Druids as the builders of Stonehenge.

According to Celtic lore, Druidism was established (under Hu Gadarn, the Mighty) in three orders: Druids, Bards and Ovates. Each was delegated different duties. To be admitted to the order, a candidate was required to be of a good family and of high moral character.

The lowest of the three divisions was the Ovate (Ovydd). They were believed to have dressed in green (an ancient emblem of innocence and youth) and under the supervision of a Druid, studied the properties of nature and assisted in sacrificial ceremonies.

The second division was that of Bard (Beirdd). They were supposed to have dressed in brown and during religious ceremonies in a sky-blue robe with a cowl. The color blue, an emblem of the heavens and the sea, may have represented truth and harmony. The Bards, whose function was to cultivate the art of music and poetry as well as literature, are referred to, by Strabo the Greek geographer and historian (63 B.C.), as "hymn makers." They were responsible for the musical part of the worship services.

These poets were held in high esteem by the Britains; for in their primeval civilization, musicians were like messengers from heaven who spoke in a language that, alone, could banish anxiety and bring contentment to a troubled heart. The Druid Bards survived the merging of Druidism into Christianity for centuries and enjoyed their ancient honors and privileges in many places down to the reign of Queen Elizabeth.

The harp, or lyre, usually pictured with the Bard, by Renaissance artists, is the primitive British or Irish harp. It was triangular in shape and strung with three strands of woven human hair. David may have played on just such a harp when he soothed the spirit of Saul, the King, and caused his wrath to depart.

The third division of Druidism was that of Druid (Derwyddon). These were the intellectual philosophers and physicians who directed the machinery of the state and the priesthood. No one could hold office who had not been educated by the Druids. On each seventh day (like the early Hebrew patriarchs) they preached to the people from small round eminences. Several of these eminences can still be seen in Britain.

English literary sources give us six successive degrees of the Druidic Order. Each degree was differentiated by the color of their sashes. They were always dressed in long robes which descended to the feet while the robes of the lower orders were only knee length.

73

The Druidic robe was white, to symbolize purity, a color they also used to symbolize the sun. Instead of sandals they wore wooden shoes of a pentagonal shape. Around their necks they wore golden torques or neckpieces.

Most descriptions indicate their hair was worn short and their beards long, whereas the lesser orders were clean shaven. The Britons, in general, wore moustaches on their upper lips, and their hair long.

The highest degree and spiritual head of the organization was the Arch-Druid. It is believed there were usually two Arch-Druids in Britain, one residing on the Isle of Anglesea and the other on the Isle of Man.(The Gildas MS, Cottonian Library, lists three Arch-Druids in Britain)   There may have been other Arch-Druids in Gaul.

The robe of the Arch-Druid is described as extremely ornate and embellished with gold, having a Cymric or Tau Cross, wrought in gold, down the length of the back. They also wore a tiara or crown of gold, embossed with a number of points to represent the sun's rays and a breastplate of the same metal.

A BRITISH DRUID

Traditional Irish lore says that the Arch-Druid generally carried a golden scepter and on special occasions his head was surmounted by a garland of oak leaves. The Arch-Druid also had other symbolical implements, such as a peculiarly shaped golden sickle with which he cut the mistletoe from the oak.

The Druids are said to have founded forty universities, having at one time an enrollment of over sixty thousand students. The Druids and Bards received up to 20 years of training in the tenents and moral teachings of their orders. Three severe examinations, held in three consecutive years, had to be successfully completed before the candidate received full initiation into the highest grades.

Every king had his Druid and Bard attached to his court. The Druidic priest or "teacher of wisdom" not only directed the education of the youthful members of the court but was allowed to instruct other pupils. He traveled through the realm often accompanied by his students. The chief Bard seems to have had a number of assistants of various degrees, who had not yet arrived at the highest achievement of their profession.

While no literary documents exist to prove the date of the establishment of Druidism in Britain, the educational system adopted by the Druids is traced to about 1800 B.C., when Hu Gadarn Hyscion (Isaacson?) or "Hu the Mighty," led a party of settlers from Asia Minor to Britain. A descendant of Abraham, Hu the Mighty's coming to Britain provides one of the first recorded instances of the fulfillment of the prophecy found in Genesis 28:14; that the "seed" of Abraham would spread abroad, to the four points of the compass.

The Welsh triads, or "traditional chronicles," give evidence of Hu the Mighty coming from Asia Minor. In the Welsh Triad 4, we read that: "The first of the three chieftains who established the colony was Hu, the Mighty, who came with the original settlers. They came over the Hazy Sea from the summer country, which is called Defrobani, that is where Constinoblys now stands."

Through his investigations (made over 200 years ago), the English antiquarian, William Stukely, asserts that true Druidism was introduced into Britain from Bible lands about the period of Abraham. He further states it was undoubtedly derived from the original, indefiled, religion of the patriarchs.

Many other authorities have noted the resemblance between the Druidic religion and that of the Old Testament. To quote Charles Hulbert, a noted British scholar: "So near is the resemblance between the Druidic religion of Britain and the patriarchal religion of the Hebrews, that we hesitate not to pronounce their origin the same." The patriarchal religion, to which Hulbert refers, consisted of family centered worship with the head of the family acting in the capacity of priest while doing the service of sacrifice.

Apparently, most present-day scholars consider such conclusions absurd and imaginary. One modern writer refers to a time "when the Biblical pedigree of the ancient European barbarians was being explored and invented;" yet in the same works he discusses "curious links" with Central Asia, an area that was occupied for a time during the westward movements of the Hebrew-Phoenicians after the Flood.

While there is admittedly little direct evidence of the Biblical origin of Druidism, the many parallelisms and similarities cannot be dismissed with sarcasm and contempt. Rather, they would indicate a need for more research and study. It is true that Stukely (and other writers of his time) did err in advocating the Druids of the Celtic period as being the builders of Stonehenge. This, in itself, is not justifiable grounds to discredit all his works.

English literature is full of references to the "pagan religious customs" of the Druids. The early writers describe the Druids as "soothsayers," performing religious rites and practices in which the planets, trees and stones were given Divine honors. However, this is only describing the idolatrous worship of the Celtic Druids. As they migrated through Europe into the British Isles, they brought with them that which is today erroneously described as "Druidism."

Although the Druids performed idolatrous ceremonies to the stars, to the elements, to hills and to trees, they never thoroughly forsook the worship of the Supreme God of all nature. In fact, it is quite possible that the Druids paid honors, rather than adoration, to their many deities. We also now know that some practices of "occult" and "magic arts" ascribed to the Druids, consisted, for the most part, of no more than a thorough knowledge of nature and some of the sciences, including astronomy.

However, over the centuries there has developed a literary record of an entire system of Druid practices, now so entwined with Celtic occult belief and folklore, that it has all but obliterated the original philosophy of Druidism.

We have a great amount of comparative evidence showing the close relationship between Druidism and the faith of the Old Testament which gives validity to the story of Hu Gadarn introducing the patriarchal faith to Britain. Centuries later, this pure theology was merged into the religion of the Celts; traces of which can still be recognized.

One outstanding comparison is the altars of the Celtic Druids which were constructed of unhewn stones, for by Druidic law it was ordained that no axe should touch the sacred stones. This precept, which gave rise to the "sacred stone worship" of the Druids, actually coincides with the Mosaic law: *"If thou with make me an altar of stone, thou shalt not build it of hewn stone."* (Exod. 20:25) Sometimes the stones were annointed with rose oil, as Jacob annointed the first stone monument on record – that which he raised as a memorial at Bethel. (Gen. 28:18)

While officiating at the altar, the priest would lay his hand on the animal to be sacrificed, making a confession of sin. Then the animal was slain, and offered as a burnt sacrifice. These ancient Druids believed expiation followed this sacrificial act; a belief which was an exact parallel to the Hebrew doctrine of blood atonement.

The Druids also held the doctrine of the immortality of the soul. Caesar, in his "Commentaries" wrote: "The Druids make the immortality of the soul the basis of all their teaching, holding it to be the principal incentive for a virtuous life." Pomponius Mela, writing about A.D. 41, affirms: "The bravery of the Britons is due to their doctrine of the immortality of the soul." Undoubtedly, Druidism was the strength of the British resistance to the Romans, who failed in their attempts to completely destroy it.

While apparently accepting sun worship and other pagan practices, the Druids worshipped the true One God, Who was Truine in Nature; Who portrayed the triple aspect of past, present and future. He was the Creator of the past, the Saviour of the present and the Renovator of the future. They believed His real name to be an indescribable mystery, as was His nature. They reasoned — "Nid dim on d duw; nid duw ond dim." (God cannot be matter; what is not matter must be God.)

The Druids revered the oak tree as a symbol of Almighty God, as did the Hebrew Patriarchs. It was underneath the oaks of Mamre that Abraham "dwelt" a long time; where he erected an altar to God, and where he received the three angels. It was underneath an oak that

Jacob hid the idols of his children (Gen. 35:4) because oaks were held to be sacred and inviolate.

ABRAHAM'S OAK NEAR HEBRON

Because mistletoe grew upon the oak, it became sacred to the Druids and was held symbolic of the coming Deliverer or "Branch." Mistletoe was known as the "All Heal," a title which bears a strange resemblance to the words of Malachi's prophecy concerning the "Sun" who should "rise with healing in His wings." This "Branch" was not only foretold by the prophets of ancient Israel but was sung also by the poets of classic antiquity. Virgil mentions "the golden branch," and Homer speaks of the "golden rod" or "branch." A parallel can be seen in the writings of three of the Old Testament prophets — Isaiah, Jeremiah and Zechariah — referring to the coming Messiah as "the Branch."

It is of interest to note that the Druids revered a form of the cross. It was their custom to search diligently for a large, handsome oak tree, having two large armlike branches. When viewed in conjunction with the trunk of the tree they formed a cross. This "cross" was then consecrated by cutting characters for the word "Hesus," spelled "Yesu," upon the right branch. Upon the middle trunk they cut the word, 'Taranus," upon the left branch, "Belenus," and over them all the word "Than," meaning God.

"Hesus" or Yesu was the Supreme God whom they worshipped as the great "All-Heal" and they believed in Him as the "Saviour" of the world. In both the Druidic religion and the Hebrew religion of patriarchal times we can see a parallel preparation for the coming of Christ. The Old Testament prophets proclaimed that the promised Messiah would come as a babe, grow to be a great teacher, and finally be revealed as the Redeemer.

Through the ministry of the Druids, the same doctrines were believed, with the expectation of the same Saviour, Hesus (Jesus). In the ancient British tongue, "Jesus" had never assumed its Greek, Latin or Hebrew form, but remained the pure Druidic "Hesus" or "Yesu." Talisen, a Welsh bard of the sixth century wrote: "Christ, the Word from the beginning was in the beginning our Teacher, and we never lost His teachings. Christianity was a new thing in Asia, but there never was a time when the Druids of Britain held not its doctrines."

Other clues, showing close relationship between Druidism and the patriarchal religion of the Old Testament, are seen in that each had a High Priest with a breastplate of similar description. Both had a priesthood exempt from taxation and military service. Both religions taught the Mosaic account of the Creation.

HIGH PRIEST

Despite its practice of pagan rites in "high places" and "sacred groves," it was the Druidic faith, rooted in Druidism, that nurtured the essential divine truths and prepared Britain for the Gospel of

Jesus Christ. When Christianity reached Britain, Druidism merged with it. Many of the Druidic priesthood became ministers in the early Christian Church. They went on to carry the message of Christianity to the far nations of the world.

This is not to imply that every individual Druid and Bard accepted Christianity on its first promulgation in Britain. Even after Christianity became the national religion of Britain, Druidism did not entirely cease until several centuries after Christ.

ARCH DRUID IN HIS JUDICIAL HABIT

''Through time with silver locks adorn'd his head
Erect his gesture yet, and firm his tread...
His seemly beard, to grace his form bestow'd
Descending decent, on his bosom flow'd
His robe a purest white, though rudely join'd
Yet showed an emblem of the purest mind.''

Anon.

TRIADS

As was customary in most schools of the Mysteries, Druidic teaching was divided into two distinct sections. The simpler, a moral code, was taught to all the people, while the deeper esoteric doctrine was given only to initiated priests.

A complete circle of Druidic training required a candidate to master mathematics, geometry, medicine, jurisprudence, poetry, oratory, natural philosophy and astronomy. The latter two subjects required in-depth study. Much of the teaching was committed to memory. The religious subject material was memorized in its entirety.

The Druidic precepts (some 20,000 in number) were all in spoken verse as it was forbidden to write them down. Consequently, the novice spent a considerable length of time in a state of probation. This Druidic practice resembled that of the Hebrews, who, although they had received the written law through Moses, maintained a certain code of precept among them which taught only by word of mouth. This mode of teaching by memory was practiced by the early Egyptians (Hebrew-Phoenician) as well as their kinsmen, the Spartans, who esteemed it better to imprint the law on the minds of their citizens than to engrave it upon tablets.

Owing to this system of learning we have only the meager evidence of the ancient authors, some fragments of Irish and Welsh literature and folk-memory. What has been found written is believed, by some scholars, to be the oldest literature in the oldest living language in Europe. Unfortunately, only a small portion has been translated and published in English.

One of the most important sources of our present-day knowledge of the Druids are the Celtic and Welsh Triads. In them, all national events were recorded and their accuracy has never been questioned. In the following verses, we find the spiritual character of Druidic teachings:
"Let God be praised in the beginning and the end,
Who supplicates Him, He will neither despise nor refuse.
God above us, God before us, God possessing (all things).
May the Father of Heaven grant us a portion of mercy!"

The Druidic doctrine of the Trinity is expressed in these verses:
"There are Three Primeval Unities, and more than one of each cannot exist: one God, one Truth and one Point of Liberty, where all opposites preponderate."
"Three things proceed from the Three Primeval Unities: all of life, all that is Good, and all Power."

The moral philosophy of the Druids, like the proverbs of the Scriptures, expresses a kind of practical wisdom to give plain guidance in daily living:

"The three foundations of Druidism: Peace, Love, Justice."

"The three primary principles of Wisdom: wisdom to the laws of God; concern for the welfare of mankind; suffering with fortitude all the accidents of life."

"Three duties of every man; worship God; be just to all men; die for your country."

"In three things will be seen the primary qualities of the soul of man: in what he may fear; what he would conceal; and what he would show."

"There are three men that all ought to look on with affection: he that with affection looks on the face of the earth; he that is delighted with rational works of art; and he that looks lovingly on little infants."

"Three things that make a man equal to an angel: the love of every good; the love of exercising charity; the love of pleasing God."

Druidic teachings concerning crime and punishment held:

"In creation there is no evil which is not a greater good than an evil. The things called rewards or punishments are so secured by eternal ordinances that they are not consequences but properties of our acts and habits. Except for crimes against society, the measure of punishment should be that which nature itself deals to the delinquent. Perfect penitence is entitled to pardon. That penitence is perfect, which makes the utmost compensation in its power for wrong inflicted, and willingly submits to the penalty prescribed. The atonement of penitents, who voluntarily submit themselves to death in expiation of guilt incurred is perfect. The souls of all such pass on to the higher cycles of existence."

Other Druidic doctrines taught:

"The three foundations of learning: seeing much; studying much; and suffering much."

"The three foundations of judgments: bold design; frequent practice; and frequent mistakes."

"The three foundations of happiness: a suffering with contentment; a hope that it will come; and a belief that it will be."

"The three foundations of thought: perspicuity; amplitude; and preciseness."

"The three qualifications of poetry: endowment of genius; judgment from experience; and happiness of mind."

"The three canons of perspicuity: the word that is necessary; the quantity that is necessary; and the manner that is necessary."

"The three canons of amplitude: appropriate thought; variety of thought; and requisite thought."

"God consists necessarily of Three Things: the Greatest of Life, the Greatest of Knowledge, and the Greatest of Power, and of what is the Greatest there can be no more than one of anything."

Druidic philosophical doctrine stated:
"Matter is the creation of God. Without God it cannot exist. Nature is the action of God through the medium of matter."

"The universe is matter as ordered and systematized by the intelligence of God. It was created by God's pronouncing His own name - at the sound of which light and the heaven sprang into existence. The name of God is itself a creative power. What in itself that name is, is known to God only. All music or natural melody is a faint and broken echo of the creative name."

"The three things God alone can do: endure the eternities of infinity; participate of all being without changing, renew everything without annihilating it."

"The justice of God cannot be satisfied except by the sacrifice of life in lieu of life."

The institutional triads were as follows:

"The three primary privileges of the Bards of the Island of Britain are: Maintenance wherever they go; that no naked weapon be borne in their presence; and their testimony preferred to all others."

"The three ultimate intentions of Bardism: to reform morals and custom; to secure peace; and to celebrate the praise of all that is good and excellent."

Three things are forbidden to the Bard: Immorality; to satirize; and to bear arms."

"The three joys of the Bards of Britain: the increase of knowledge; the reformation of manners; and the triumphs of peace over the lawless and depredators."

The Druidic teaching concerning a man's spiritual nature:
"In every person there is a soul
In every soul there is intelligence
In every intelligence there is thought
In every thought there is either good or evil
In every evil there is death
In every good there is life
In every life there is God."

STONES 57, 58 AND 158 AFTER RE-ERECTION IN 1958

THE ORIGIN OF THE CELTIC DRUIDS

It is well established that the British Celts were a part of the great Celtic expansion that took place in the third century B,C, During this period, the inhabitants of Central and West Europe spread from Iberia in the west to the Carpathians and the borders of the Ukraine in the east, with Galatian colony being their most easterly outpost. They moved southward to the Alps and parts of northern Italy and northwards into the British Isles.

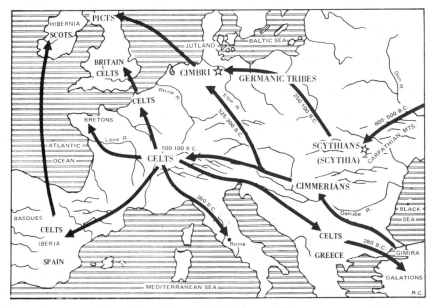

However, the origin of these inhabitants of Europe was not known, with certainty, until recent years. Archaeological findings have now established, unquestionably, that the Celts (and Gauls) were the main body of Cimmerians who came out of Asia Minor. Originally, they were the people the Assyrians called "Gimira" and "Iskuza;" earlier they were known as "Khumri." (Ghomri) Khumri, a name derived from Omri, one of the kings of the Northern Kingdom of Israel, has been found on a stone monument, known as the "Black Obelisk." Khumri was the Assyrian name for the Israelites who had been taken into Assyrian captivity in 721 B.C. These people became the so-called "Lost Tribes of Israel."

The Scythians have likewise been traced to the same Gimira people, or Israelites. The Scythians were the Israelites who migrated north, through the Caucasus into the steppe regions of South Russia. From there, centuries later, they traveled west into the Carpathians, west of the Black Sea, to establish themselves as the great and prosperous kingdom of Scythia.

Two great mysteries have been solved by the above findings: the origin of countless thousands of Scythians and Cimmerians and the destiny of countless thousands of Israelites who vanished, both at the same time in history.

The Scythians and Cimmerians who developed into the Anglo-Saxon, Scandinavian, Germanic, Lombardic and Celtic nations were the Israelite tribes prophesied in the Scriptures to be spread "among the heathen." Later, they were to move into a new land; the "appointed place;" the Isles of the sea in the north and west where they were to embrace the faith of Christ (nationally) and became His witnesses throughout the world. (A detailed study of the migrations of Israel can be found in "King Solomon's Temple" by this author — (see listing inside back cover)

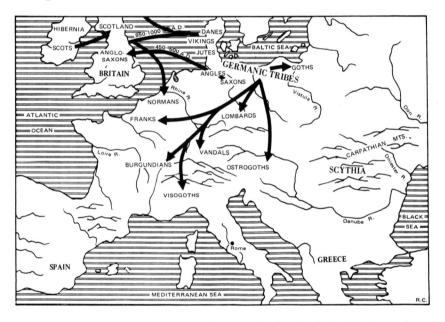

Thus, we find that centuries before the birth of Christ, the tribes of Israel (who were to be blind to their identity — Hos. 1:9; Isa. 42:16; Rom. 11:25) followed the "waymarks" of their kinsmen Hebrew-Phoenicians who had built Stonehenge (centuries earlier) and established Druidism as the national religion of Britain.

The pagan, idolatrous worship that the Celtic Druids brought with them, which today is described as "Druidism," is additional evidence of their relationship with ancient Israel. This was due to their imitating the idolatrous practices of the peoples through which they migrated. A study of the Scriptures shows the worship practices of pre-Christian Celtic Britain and pre-captivity Israel as being almost identical. Both worshipped Baal. Both built temples to him in the groves, by the oak trees, and on high places. Gaulish Druids may have performed human sacrifices on their altars as did the Israelites. (Jer. 19:5)

It was during the time that Solomon was king over Israel that the religious life of the Israel nation began to decline: *"For it came to pass, when Solomon was old, that his wives turned away his heart after other gods: and his heart was not perfect with the Lord his God, as was the heart of David his father. For Solomon went after Ashtoreth the goddess of the Zidonians, and after Milcom the abomination of the Ammonites. And Solomon did evil in the sight of the Lord, and went not fully after the Lord, as did David his father. Then did Solomon build an high place for Chemosh, the abomination of Moab, in the hill that is before Jerusalem, and for Molech, the abomination of Ammon. And likewise did he for all his strange wives, which burnt incense and sacrificed unto their gods."* (I Kings 11:4-8)

A century later brought the utter corruption of the Israel nation as Ahab, the son of Omri,*"...did evil in the sight of the Lord above all that were before him...that he took to wife Jezebel the daughter of Ethbaal king of the Zidonians, and went and served Baal, and worshipped him. And he reared up an altar for Baal in the house of Baal, which he had built in Samaria. And Ahab made a grove; and Ahab did more to provoke the Lord God of Israel to anger than all the kings of Israel that were before him."* (I Kings 16:31-33)

It was their continued idolatry, their pagan worship of Baal, the sun-god, in their high places that precipitated the overthrow of the Kingdom of Israel in 721 B.C. and their captivity by the Assyrians; *"...And they left all the commandments of the Lord their God, and made them molten images, even two calves, and made a grove, and worshipped all the host of heaven, and served Baal. And they caused their sons and their daughters to pass through the fire, and used divination and enchantments, and sold themselves to do evil in the sight of the Lord, to provoke him to anger. Therefore the Lord was very angry with Israel, and removed them out of His sight: there was none left but the tribe of Judah only."* (II Kings 17:16-18)

The southern part of Israel, known as the Kingdom of Judah, continued to practice idolatry and were, in turn, taken captive to Assyria to be joined with the northern Kingdom of Israel in bondage. The only exceptions were the inhabitants of the city of Jerusalem, in 539 B.C., to set up the heterogeneous nation of the Jews.

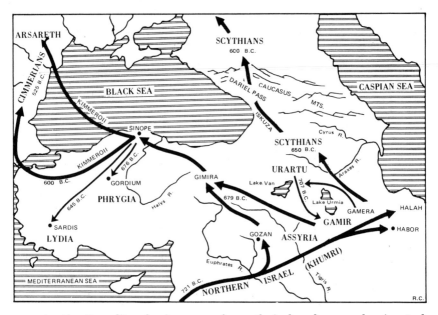

As the Israelites broke away from their bondage and migrated west, the Bible specifically states that the Israelites continued to profane the Lord's name among the heathen. *"And I scattered them among the heathen, and they were dispersed through the countries: according to their way and according to their doings I judged them... they profaned my holy name, when they said to them, These are the people of the Lord, and are gone forth out of His land. But I had pity for Mine holy name, which the house of Israel had profaned among the heathen, whither they went. Therefore say unto the house of Israel, Thus saith the Lord God: I do not this for your sakes, O house of Israel, but for Mine holy name's sake, which ye have profaned among the heathen, whither ye went. And I will sanctify My great name...and the heathen shall know that I am the Lord, saith the Lord God, when I shall be sanctified in you before their eyes."* (Ezekiel 36 . 19-23)

The latter part of this prophecy to the Kingdom of Israel began its fulfillment as the Druidic priesthood in Britain accepted Christianity. A further fulfillment occurred when the United States of America was founded in 1776 A.D. as a Christian nation. A far greater fulfillment has yet to take place . (Jer. 31:31-34)

The prevailing belief, held by most Theologians, is that the tribes of Israel, taken to Assyria, became assimilated among the heathen and thus were lost forever. This theory is profoundly inconsistent with Ezekiel's prophecy. The prophet clearly states that God was to deal with the Israelites as a people, after their captivity, in a new homeland.

STELLAR REVELATION

When it is understood that the builders of Stonehenge were descendants of the Hebrew-Phoenicians, the mystery of Stonehenge is solved. Stonehenge, as well as scores of other stone circles and avenues in Britain, was designed to observe the heavens. The Universe was the "Bible" of the early British astronomer-priests, as it was of the ancient Hebrews. They recognized that the Celestial creation contained revelations from God.

The Psalmist said: "The heavens declare the Glory of God, and the firmament showeth His handiwork." All the major constellations, planets and stars were examined with a view to deciphering their message to man. It was such sightings that guided the "Wise Men" to the cradle of the Saviour, to worship the "Star" which was to rise out to Jacob; (Num. 24:17) "the Sun of Righteousness" which the Prophet Malachi had foretold some 500 years before. (Mal. 4:2)

In the Book of Job (generally believed to be the oldest book in the Bible) we have many references to this "Stellar Revelation." This would be at least 2000 years before Christ. In Job, the signs of the

Zodiac and the names of several stars and constellations are mentioned as being both ancient and well known. In Psalms 147:4, we read: *"He telleth the number of the stars; He giveth them all their names."* R.V.).

These ancient star-pictures were designed to preserve, expound, and perpetuate a record of how God would deal with mankind, from the foundation of the world to the end of time as we know it. Pictures speak in every language, to all people everywhere. By this means, God revealed Himself and His plans to mankind before the Bible was written, and even before the Great Pyramid of Egypt (The Bible in Stone) was built.

The Zodiacal Circle is an imaginary band encircling the heavens through which our solar system revolves. It is divided into twelve divisions, or "signs," named for the constellations, which are regions in the sky or celestial sphere. Each "sign" is associated with three "constellations" making a total of 48 "star-pictures."

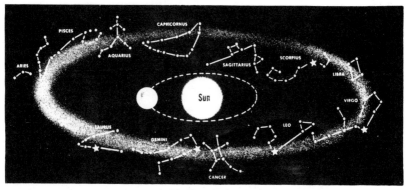

Zodiac Belt

The figures themselves are entirely arbitrary. There is nothing in the groups of stars to even suggest the figures, yet if we turn to history and tradition, we find that the Twelve Signs are consistent. They conform as to the meaning of their names and as to their order, in all the Zodiacs of the ancient world. The Chinese, Chaldean and Egyptian records go back to a period before 2,000 B.C. The Egyptian Zodiacs found in the Temples of Denderah and Esneh, appear, from internal evidence, to be copies of Zodiacs from nearly 4,000 B.C., when the summer soltice was in the sign Leo.

The ancient star names and pictures, which have come down to us, are still preserved in every good celestial atlas. Therefore, the pictures are the originals. They must have been drawn around or connected with certain stars, so that picture and star formations might be identified and associated. In this manner, a pictorial record was preserved and handed down to posterity.

Ancient Persian and Arabian traditions ascribe the invention of the Zodiac to Adam, Seth and Enoch. Josephus asserts that it originated in the family of Seth. Nouet, a French astronomer infers that the Egyptian Astronomy (Zodiacal) must have arisen around 5,400 B.C.; a date Bible Chronologists have established as contemporary with Adam. The pre-Adamic peoples of Egypt and elsewhere have been assigned knowledge of astronomy in esoteric writings but no archaeological evidence has ever been found to substantiate this hypothesis.

The twelve "signs" of the Zodiac constitute twelve graphic chapters in a picturesque "book" of Divine revelation. The cast of characters begins with Virgo, the Virgin, and climaxes with Leo, the Lion. The overall panorama illustrates the visual story of the Redeemer, born as the Seed of a virgin. After being wounded, He returns as the Coming One, to bruise the serpent's head (Gen. 3:15) and to judge and rule in righteousness. (Rev. 19:11, 15, 16) Each of the remaining signs of the Zodiac portrays the many details of this celestial message.

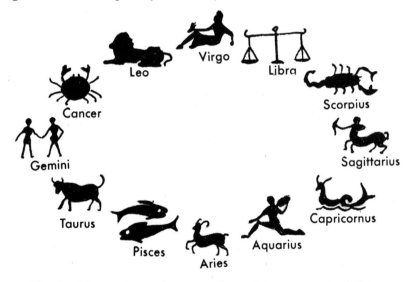

The Scriptures themselves are the written account of this same celestial revelation. They are not (as is often suggested) an evolutionary development of the world's ancient religions which were often corruptions and perversions of primitive truths.

In our day, the stars, so constant and dependable, still carry forward the record entrusted to them. For a detailed study of how the star formations witness to the accuracy of Biblical prophecy, the reader is directed to read "The Glory of the Stars" (see listing inside back cover).

THE SUNRISE TRILITHON

For many hundreds of years the high priests of Druidism gathered at Stonehenge to witness the sunrise on the day of the Winter solstice. On that day each year, as viewed from the inside of the stone circle, the sunrise is visible through a narrow opening between the trilithon stones number 51 and 52, known as the "Sunrise Trilithon."

When the sun has risen just enough so that it appears to be sitting of the horizon, its apparent diameter fits exactly the distance between the two great stones. In so doing, the sun marks the beginning of the shortest day of the year, the astronomical ending of the old and the beginning of the new year.

At that instant, the sun's full rays coming through the narrow space between the two upright stones, radiate in eight rays, forming a perfect crossed cross. Such a cross is also produced by overlaying the letters x (aleph) and + (tau), the first and last letters of the original Hebrew alphabet.

In fact that God manifests Himself in light (Psalm 104:1, 2 — I John 1:5) and that under certain conditions light appears as a crossed cross, added to the significance of the "aleph" and "tau," clearly indicates that a crossed cross is a symbol of the Everlastingness of

God. *"Thus saith the Lord King of Israel, and his redeemer the Lord of hosts; I am the first, and I am the last; and besides me there is no God."* (Isa. 44:6) *"Hearken unto me, O Jacob and Israel, my called: I am he; I am the first I also am the last."* (Isa. 48:12)

Significantly, the first and last letters of the Hebrew alphabet form the name of God in the Old Testament. In the New Testament the first and last letters of the Greek alphabet, "Alpha" and "Omega," are used by our Lord as a name for Himself. Thus Christ is declaring that He and God are One, the beginning and the end, the first and the last of all things; *"Saying, I am Alpha and Omega, the first and the last ..."* (Rev. 1:11) *"And he said unto me, It is done. I am Alpha and Omega, the beginning and the end, the first and the last."* (Rev. 22:13)

It has long been recognized in studying the symbolism of Bible numbers that the number eight is the number of Christ. With this thought in mind, consider the rather sudden adoption, in modern times, of the crossed cross as the form of the Christmas Star. This eight-rayed star is found pictured on Christmas greeting cards, seals and stamps of different countries.

These questions come to mind. Is this crossed star the true form of the Christmas "Star" which appeared to the Wise Men or "Magi" and led them to the Christ Child? Is this crossed star to be the true form of the "sign of the Son of man" which is to appear in the heavens, as a "sign" or herald, announcing our Lord's return? *"And then shall appear the sign of the Son of man in heaven: and then shall all the tribes of the earth mourn, and they shall see the Son of man coming in the clouds of heaven with power and great glory."* (Matt. 24:30)

The Druidic symbol of the Trinity.

THE DRUID'S PRAYER

Grant, O God thy protection
And in protection, strength
And in Strength, understanding
And in understanding, knowledge
And in knowledge, the knowledge of justice
And in the knowledge of justice, the love of it
And in that love, the love of all existence
And in that love of all existence
The love of God, and all goodness

(Translated from the Welsh language)

"Remove not the ancient landmark, which thy fathers have set."
Proverbs 22:28

ACKNOWLEDGEMENT

It is hoped that through reading this modest introduction to Stonehenge, the reader will be motivated to a deeper study of this unique monument and the race of people who built it, leading to a new understanding of our kinship with the people of the Book.

The astronomical features and illustrated charts of Stonehenge, used in this treatise, are based on the works of astronomer Dr. Gerald S. Hawkins. (Stonehenge Decoded – Doubleday and Co., New York)

Illustrations of megalithic monuments and extracts, relating to the "waymarks" of the megalithic builders, were taken from the "Bible Research Handbook."(Covenant Publishing Co., Ltd., London, G.B.)

Geometric relationship between the Sacred Cubit and the Royal Cubit taken from Pyramidology Book I — Dr. Adam Rutherford, F.R.A.S.,F.R.G.S. (Institute of Pyramidology, Great Britain)

The relationship between an eight pointed star (or sunlight appearing as a crossed cross) and symbolism of Jesus Christ was first suggested by W.H. Bennett, a Canadian Bible lecturer, in 1967.

This treatise is also indebted to Professor R.J.C. Atkinson, Department of Archaeology, University College, Cardiff; Professor Alexander Thom, Emeritus of Engineering, University of Oxford; Department of the Environment, Great Britain.

E. Raymond Capt

An Ode to Druidism

"Out of monuments, names, proverbs, traditions, private records and evidences, fragments of story, passages of books and the like,we do save and recover somewhat from the deluge of time."

Bacon